W9-CHX-905

Magnificent Spiral
Mandala Quilts

RaNae Merrill

kp

KRAUSE PUBLICATIONS
CINCINNATI, OHIO

www.fwmedia.com

14 13 12 11 10   5 4 3 2 1

Distributed in Canada by Fraser Direct
100 Armstrong Avenue
Georgetown, ON, Canada L7G 5S4
Tel: (905) 877-4411

Distributed in the U.K. and Europe by F+W Media International
Brunel House, Newton Abbot, Devon, TQ12 4PU, England
Tel: (+44) 1626 323200, Fax: (+44) 1626 323319
Email: postmaster@davidandcharles.co.uk

Distributed in Australia by Capricorn Link
P.O. Box 704, S. Windsor NSW, 2756 Australia
Tel: (02) 4577-3555

Library of Congress Cataloging in Publication Data
Merrill, RaNae.
  Magnificent spiral mandala quilts / RaNae Merrill.
    p. cm.
  Includes index.
  ISBN 978-1-4402-0425-8 (alk. paper)
  1. Patchwork–Patterns. 2. Quilting–Patterns.
3. Spirals in art. I. Title.
  TT835.M4792 2010
  746.46'041–dc22
                          2010014832

About the Author

RaNae Merrill found her calling as a professional quilter after previous careers as a pianist, a photographer and a travel writer. These days she satisfies her wanderlust by traveling to quilt shows and guilds as a teacher and lecturer. She has designed fabrics for Blank Quilting and has published patterns in a variety of quilt magazines. RaNae's first book, *Simply Amazing Spiral Quilts* (Krause), is a quilting best seller. This is her second (but probably not her last) book.

Metric Conversion Chart

To convert	to	multiply by
Inches	Centimeters	2.54
Centimeters	Inches	0.4
Feet	Centimeters	30.5
Centimeters	Feet	0.03
Yards	Meters	0.9
Meters	Yards	1.1

Edited by **Jennifer Claydon**
Designed by **Kelly O'Dell**
Production coordinated by **Greg Nock**
Photography by **Ric Deliantoni** and
          Christine Polomsky

Acknowledgments

Thanks to:

- The wonderful quilters who saw me through the process of drafting, revising and refining my teaching techniques, and in the process designed and made most of the quilts in this book. I could not have done this without you.

Amy Dawdy	Dwight, Illinois
Anita Mester	Austin, Texas
Barbara Baker	Meadow Vista, California
Betsy Vinegrad	Short Hills, New Jersey
Daniel Lundby	Marion, Iowa
Deb Sorem	Salem, Oregon
Debra Nance	Jasper, Tennessee
Dottie Lankard	Independence, Kansas
Georgianne Kandler	Arroyo Grande, California
Gill Drury	Hampshire, England
Holly Watson	Oakdale, Minnesota
Jamie McClenaghan	Fairfield, California
Jill Kerekes	Flemington, New Jersey
Kerry Hansing	Pittsburg, California
Linda Cooper	Burke, Virginia
Linda McGibbon	Beaverton, Michigan
Martha Flanagan	Clifton Park, New York
Mary Cannizaro	South Salem, New York
Mary Reddington	Springfield, Virginia
Patty Martin	Fair Oaks, California
Priscilla Roehm	Colchester, Vermont
Rhonda Adams	Alexandria, California
Robin Armstead	Copperas Cove, Texas
Ruth Shadar	Hod HaSharon, Israel
Susan Arnold	Sunnyvale, California
Susan Harmon	Cherryvale, Kansas
Susan Ott	Bradenton, Florida
Susan Wood	Madison, Connecticut

And the other quilters who, for whatever reasons, were not able to make quilts, but whose questions and feedback were invaluable in helping me formulate coherent instructions.

- Lela and Annette S., non-quilting friends who always answer their cell phones, no matter where they are, to provide much-needed distractions from writing and quilting.

- Jenni, my editor, who took the book from instruction to art, and didn't laugh at me when I planned ahead for a stress-out deadline meltdown that miraculously never came. Christine, my photographer and Kelly, my designer.

- Penny McMorris and Andrea Bishop at Electric Quilt for their help in editing the EQ instructions.

- Joanie Zeier Poole, for coaching me to a new level of machine quilting, and Terry White for sharing her Star Cotton thread with me.

- Terry Niefield and Andy Unangst, for helping out with photography.

- Joe Snyder at Singer, who provided sewing machines whenever and wherever I needed one.

- Victor, who cooked gourmet French dinners for me and while I was writing reminded me often that life isn't all work.

- Morgan, my dog, who is always at my side and who insists that I stop writing or sewing to take her for a long walk every day.

Table of Contents

On the CD

- Instructions for using the CD
- Instructions for printing files
- PDF project Files
- Quilt Binding Instructions
- Pie and Wedge Templates
- Wedge Puzzles
- Enlarging Grids
- Background Templates
- Fabric Selection Guides
- EQ information and projects

Introduction

WHAT IS A MANDALA?

Mandala (MUN-duh-luh) is the Sanskrit word for a design used to help focus meditation. Creating a mandala is considered by many people to be a form of worship. Mandala designs are often circular, and can be quite intricate. They can be made in any media and can contain any elements that the creator feels inspired to include. What makes a design special is that it carries some form of spiritual significance to the maker and, perhaps, also the viewer.

The quilts in this book are called mandala quilts for several reasons: one spiritual and others practical.

The spiritual reason for including mandala in the name is that the idea for spiral mandala quilts came to me one day while I was sitting in church looking at the round stained-glass rose window. Because of this, these quilts can carry a certain spiritual and meditative significance for me.

The practical reason for including mandala in the name is that although these designs can look kaleidoscopic, I do not want them to be confused with Paula Nadelstern's kaleidoscope quilts.

Finally, the reason for including spiral in the name is simple—these quilts are all made with spirals.

SIMPLY AMAZING SPIRAL QUILTS

Magnificent Spiral Mandala Quilts builds on the concepts I introduced in my first book, *Simply Amazing Spiral Quilts*. (I really thought I had said all I had to say about spirals. Then one morning, I woke up with this book in my head and knew there had to be a sequel.)

All of the design concepts in *Magnificent Spiral Mandala Quilts* are unique to this book. It was necessary to include in this book the fundamental information on drawing and sewing spirals that you will also find in *Simply Amazing Spiral Quilts*; however, even some of that information has been updated and improved here. *Magnificent Spiral Mandala Quilts* and *Simply Amazing Spiral Quilts* are designed to work separately, but they work even better together—you can find additional inspiration in *Simply Amazing Spiral Quilts*. Think of the two books like a good marriage: Each can stand on its own, but together they are more than the sum of the parts.

HOW TO USE THIS BOOK

If you can sew a Log Cabin block, you can make a spiral mandala quilt. One of the most wonderful things about these quilts is that when you break them down into their elements, you find that they are much simpler than they look. Making one is just a new way of applying skills you probably already have.

Magnificent Spiral Mandala Quilts is designed to be used three ways:

1. Make one of the projects in the book:
   Go to the projects on pages 120–149. Print out the foundations from the CD. Begin working from Copying Spirals for Foundations (see page 94) and follow the instructions from there through sewing the spirals and assembling the mandala.

2. Create your own design with ready-made templates:
   Use the wedge puzzle templates on the CD as building blocks to design your own original spiral mandala. Begin working at Step 2: Placing Spirals in the Wedge (see page 14) to develop your own design and coloring. Then follow the instructions in the second half of the book for sewing the quilt.

3. Design a spiral mandala completely from scratch:
   Start at the beginning. This book is written to take you step-by-step through discovering your own unique spiral mandala quilt design. Specific steps and tools guide you through the process of creating a spiral mandala. Follow these instructions exactly—even when you're instructed to close your eyes! After you see the results, I will explain what happened and why so that you can use this design tool on your own.

THE SPIROMANDALAS BLOG

During the process of writing this book, I worked with the people making the quilts displayed in this book via a private blog. Each quilter had a page where we carried on a dialogue as the design was developed. That blog is now open to the public at http://spiromandalas. wordpress.com. If you would like to better understand how a quilter arrived at her or his spiral mandala design, simply visit the blog and click on the quilter's name.

CHAPTER ONE

Designing a Spiral Mandala Quilt

This chapter will take you step by step through the process of designing a spiral mandala quilt. The exercises in this chapter are designed to help you learn by doing. At first, do the exercises without trying to control the outcome—I'll even ask you to close your eyes during one step. I ask you to work this way because you can't control what you don't yet understand. As you work through the steps, you will gain an understanding of what to expect; then, if you wish, you can take more control of the design process. To start, though, trust the exercises to guide you; the control will come later, after you've developed an understanding of the process.

Another reason I recommend not trying to control the outcome is that by letting go, you will probably surpass your own expectations, and your designs will reach another level. (I'm speaking from experience here!) This is intrinsic to the idea of a mandala: that you allow yourself to be open to something that comes from somewhere beyond yourself. Listening to this inspiration, having a dialogue with the work itself, is a great part of the fun of designing.

I have divided the design information into two sections: The first section takes you step by step through the easiest method of designing a spiral mandala. The next section provides additional detail and more advanced techniques. Dive into the more advanced section when you understand the basics and feel ready to explore greater possibilities.

Trust the process, discover your design and have fun!

Drawing a Spiral Mandala

Many quilters are accustomed to making a quilt with square blocks in rows, but spiral mandalas require a different approach. The designs here are based on a circle sliced into wedges. I call this the pie. Think of the wedges as triangular sections that join to make a circular quilt. Each wedge is divided into smaller shapes that contain spirals.

To design a spiral mandala, you will need the following items:

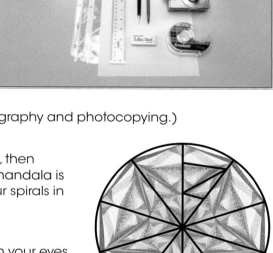

- A pie drawn on a piece of paper (These can be found on the disk included in this book.)
- A pencil (Preferably a mechanical pencil capable of drawing a fine line—my favorite is a Pentel P205.)
- An eraser
- A red pen
- A few plastic page protectors
- A straightedge (A thin ruler that lays flat on the paper is best.)
- A pair of 10"–12" square mirrors hinged together with tape
- Translucent foundation paper (See page 95 for detailed information.)
- A digital camera
- A photocopier (See page 156 for information about photography and photocopying.)

STEP 1: DIVIDING THE WEDGE

To draw a spiral mandala, start with a pie sliced into wedges, then divide the wedges into shapes. The key to a really beautiful mandala is to divide the wedge into irregular shapes that will stretch your spirals in dramatic ways.

BLIND MAN'S BLUFF

This exercise is called Blind Man's Bluff because you do it with your eyes closed. This helps you divide wedges into irregular shapes without even thinking about it. You won't be limited by your past habits and patterns, and you will discover something new in the outcome.

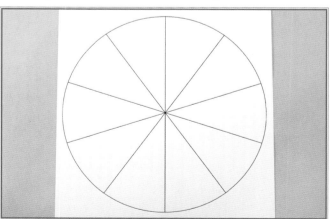

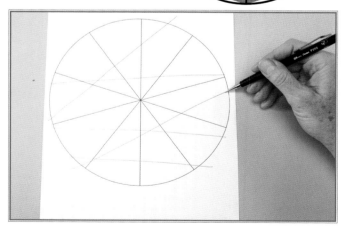

1 Select and print a pie from the CD. The first time you do this, use a pie with an even number of wedges. (The example here has 10 wedges.) Place the pie on the table in front of you.

2 Pick up the pencil. Close your eyes. Draw 4–6 straight lines across the paper, in different directions, without looking.

10

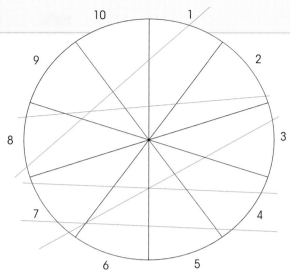

3 Open your eyes. With the red pen and the ruler, draw over the pencil lines to make them straight. Erase the pencil lines so you have a clean drawing to work with.

4 Each wedge of the pie is now divided differently into several irregular shapes; the divided wedges each form a different *wedge skeleton.* Number each wedge skeleton around the outside edge of the pie.

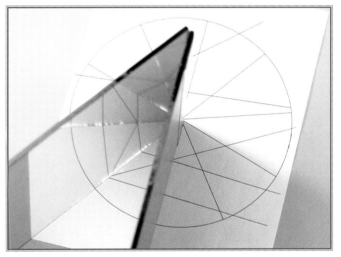

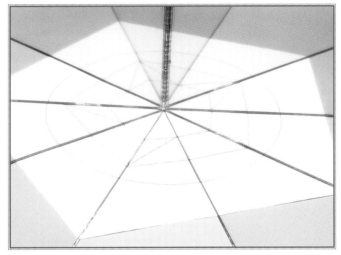

5 Each wedge skeleton in this pie is the framework of one possible mandala. (Actually more than one, but we'll get to that later.) Look at each wedge skeleton with the mirrors. To do this, place the hinge of the mirrors at the center of the pie and each mirror along one side of a wedge, as shown here.

6 The reflection in the mirror shows that wedge skeleton as the framework of a complete mandala with mirror symmetry. (We'll talk more about symmetry later on pages 26–41). Even though this is only the *mandala skeleton,* looking at it now with the mirrors helps you begin to envision a circular design.

TIP

You can also place the mirrors so that two or more adjacent wedges—up to half of the pie—are reflected together. This creates mandalas with compound mirror symmetry. (We'll explore that on pages 30–31.)

You now have as many mandala skeletons as you have wedges in your pie; for instance, if your pie has 10 wedges, you have 10 mandala skeletons. Here are some of the mandala skeletons from the 10 wedges on the previous page.

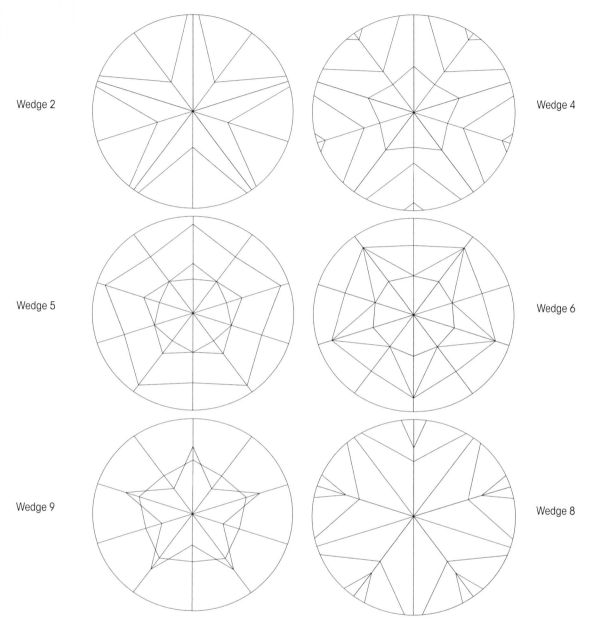

Wedge 2

Wedge 4

Wedge 5

Wedge 6

Wedge 9

Wedge 8

Once you have looked at all of the wedges with the mirrors, choose one for your mandala. How do you know which one? It's a bit of a guess because you don't know how the mandala will look with spirals in it at this point, but here are some guidelines.

- Choose a wedge with interesting shapes—different proportions, different sizes.
- Choose a wedge where the shapes are distributed evenly throughout the wedge.
- If this is your first spiral mandala, choose a wedge with no more than 4 shapes.

For the examples that follow, I'll use the Wedge 6, highlighted in red here. It is the wedge used in *Crest of the Crane*, page 120.

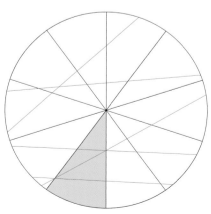

Don't try to predict a mandala

Don't start with a picture and then try to make your mandala look like it—you'll most likely end up stuck. Spirals have their own language of shapes and forms, called flow forms (we'll get there in a moment, but if you really want to jump ahead, see pages 20–21). Think of creating a spiral quilt like writing a poem in "Spiralese." Learn the language and let the mandala emerge as a dialogue between yourself and the design. Even after drawing hundreds of spiral mandalas, my best designs still come when I listen and let the mandala show me its unique possibilities.

Is Blind Man's Bluff the only way to divide a wedge?

No, but it is the best way to start. It automatically creates irregular shapes in the wedges and ensures that all the shapes have corners that point out. It also avoids T-joints (see page 41). There is more information about dividing wedges on pages 32–37, but you need to master the basics here before attempting a more advanced approach.

Why divide my wedge into irregular shapes?

Irregular shapes have sides of different lengths, some shorter, some longer. Shorter sides create thin, ribbon-like spokes (the curved arms of the spiral), while longer sides produce broad, petal-like spokes. Having spokes of different proportions in your spiral mandala makes it more interesting and dramatic. As you look through the examples below and throughout this book, pay attention to the proportions of the spokes and flow forms in the spirals.

More is not always better

A good rule of thumb is to limit the number of shapes in a wedge skeleton to no more than 5 or 6. With more, not only can the design feel too busy, but the pieces become too small to sew comfortably. It is possible to create a beautiful mandala with as few as 2 spirals in a wedge (see *Supernova*, page 40; *Elizabeth*, page 128 and *Majestic Mandalai*, page 28).

Outies, not innies

Remember, when you draw a shape to contain a spiral, all the corners must point outward. Blind Man's Bluff always produces shapes with corners pointing out. If you divide a wedge another way, check the shapes for corners pointing in. (See Shapes for Spirals, page 58.) If you find one, one way to cure it is to simply divide the shape again at that corner.

Ugly wedges = beautiful mandalas

Remember that, just as in people, the skeleton of a wedge is not the pretty part. Often, the uglier the skeleton is, the more dramatic and beautiful the mandala will be. So, don't try to draw a pretty wedge skeleton or mandala skeleton.

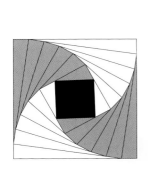
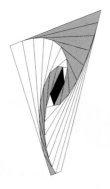
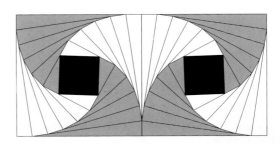
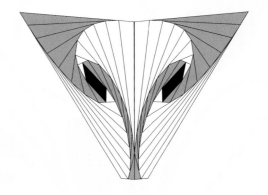

The spiral above left has four equal sides, so all the spokes are the same. The spiral above right also has four sides, but the lengths of the sides are different, so the spokes have different proportions. The difference between spirals is dramatic, and even more so when the spirals are set in mirrored symmetry as shown in the combinations at right.

STEP 2: PLACING SPIRALS IN THE WEDGE—WEDGE PUZZLES AND FLOW FORMS

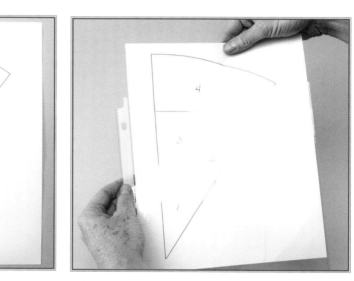

Now that you have chosen a wedge skeleton, the next step is to place spirals in the shapes inside the wedge. To do this, we'll create a *wedge puzzle* and use it to try different combinations of clockwise and counterclockwise spirals that will create different mandalas.

In a spiral mandala, each shape within the wedge contains a spiral. As you place spirals in the shapes, the spokes of adjacent spirals connect to create *flow forms*. The straight sides of the shapes disappear, and the curving, connecting flow forms become the design. It's amazing to watch the mandala suddenly change from a skeleton of straight-sided shapes to a flower-like design full of curves.

MAKE A WEDGE PUZZLE

In order to create a wedge puzzle you will need to draw spirals in each shape of your wedge. Drawing the various types of spirals is explained on pages 58–78. Skip to these pages now to learn how to draw spirals, then return here to create a wedge puzzle. For the wedge puzzle, we'll use mostly Nesting spirals (pages 61–65), with an occasional Baravelle spiral (pages 71–74) or Point-to-Point spiral (pages 75–78).

1 Use the wedge that you selected from your Blind Man's Bluff exercise. In the examples here, I'll continue using Wedge 6 from page 12.

For the wedge puzzle, you'll need a wedge skeleton that has 10" sides. Enlarge the wedge skeleton from 4" sides to 10" sides using the Enlarging Grids included on the CD, or enlarge it 250% on a photocopier. Alternatively, you can start with a single 10" wedge and divide it using the Blind Man's Bluff technique. If you do, use a 1/6, 1/8, 1/10 or 1/12 wedge until you understand the various types of symmetry. (See More on Symmetry, pages 26–41.)

Make 3 copies of the 10" wedge skeleton. Make color copies if you can so that the skeleton lines are red, or trace over the skeleton lines with a red pen. Save the original in case you want to make more copies later.

2 On the first copy of the wedge skeleton, number each shape in the wedge. Put this copy in a plastic page protector.

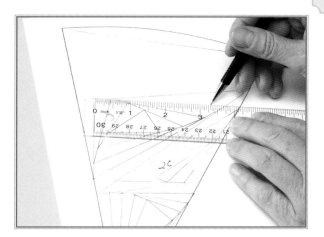

3 On the second copy of the wedge skeleton, use a pencil to draw a clockwise-spinning spiral in each shape of the skeleton. Use the same increment for every triangle in the first ring of every spiral. These spirals don't have to be perfect right now. Later, when you draft the actual full-size wedge, that's when you'll draw everything exactly as it needs to be to fit together.

What type of spiral should I place in the shapes of the wedge puzzle?

Nesting (see pages 61-65)

These are the most common spirals in mandalas. Use them in any shape with 3–6 sides. For a wedge puzzle with 10" sides, use increments of ½"–¾" when you draw Nesting spirals. Increment length doesn't have to be exact, and can vary from place to place.

Baravelle (see pages 71-74)

These spirals work in shapes with any number of sides, but are best in shapes with 6 or more sides. They function best in large shapes with fairly equal sides that give them room to spin. They are the spinniest, so use them where you want a really spirally spiral.

Point-to-Point (see pages 75-78)

These work only in shapes with 5 or more sides. Use Point-to-Point spirals in large shapes with fairly equal sides that will give them room to spin. Linked, they can create a lovely ribbon effect.

Pinwheel (see pages 67-70)

Use Nesting spirals for now since they are easier to draw and sew. Later, when you're drafting the final wedge, you might use Pinwheel spirals in some places for certain functional advantages.

Clockwise and Counterclockwise

A spiral can spin either clockwise or counterclockwise within a shape. These terms can be a bit confusing, because if you start at the center of a spiral and follow a spoke outward to the edge, the spoke curves in one direction. But, if you start at the outer edge of a spiral and follow the same spoke inward to the center, it curves in the opposite direction.

When you draw a spiral, you work from the outer edge to the center. So, we'll define the direction of the spiral as the direction the spokes curve when you travel from the outer edge toward the center. Clockwise means that the spokes curve clockwise as they travel from outer edge to center. Counterclockwise means the spokes curve counterclockwise as they travel from outer edge to center. This is consistent with the direction you mark the increment dots in a Nesting or Pinwheel spiral (see page 62); if you mark the dots clockwise from the corner of the shape, you create a clockwise-spinning spiral (and vice versa).

Since the abbreviations CW and CCW look so similar, throughout the book I'll use C for clockwise and X for counterclockwise.

Clockwise (C)   Counterclockwise (X)

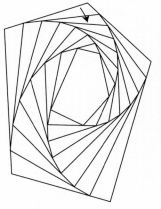
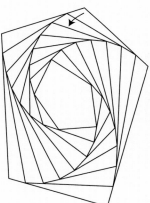

To change the direction of a spiral:

If the outer shape of a spiral is symmetrical, you can change the direction of spin simply by copying the spiral on translucent foundation paper and turning it over, or by photocopying it in mirror image.

If the outer shape of the spiral is not symmetrical (as in the examples above), to change the direction of the spiral inside the shape you must redraw the spiral in the opposite direction.

Baravelle spirals (see pages 71–74) spin equally in either direction, so to change a Baravelle from one direction to the other, simply shade the spokes in the opposite direction. You do not have to redraw the spiral.

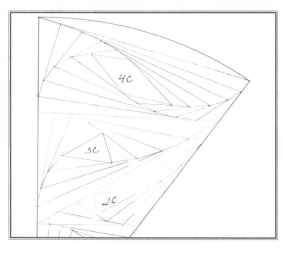

4 In the center of each spiral, write the same number as the corresponding shape on the first copy, followed by the letter C for clockwise. As you fill in the spirals, you'll start to see the straight lines disappear and the flow forms take over. Even though the straight-sided shapes disappear when you put spirals in them, they are still an important part of the mandala. The shapes are the individual spirals you sew and then join to form the wedges that become the mandala.

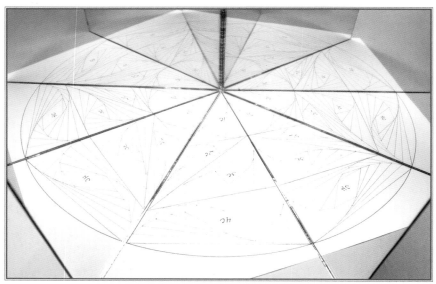

5 When you have filled each shape with a spiral, place the hinged mirrors along the sides of the wedge and watch your design bloom. Congratulations—you just created your first spiral mandala!

Since all of the spirals here spin in the same direction (clockwise), all of the flow forms are trunks (see page 20).

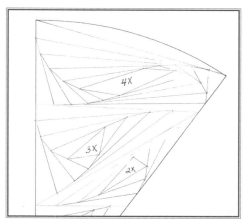

6 On the third copy of the wedge skeleton, draw a counterclockwise spiral in each shape. As before, use the same increment for every triangle in the first ring of all spirals. In the center of each spiral, write the same number as the corresponding shape on the first copy, followed by X for counterclockwise.

TIP

If you drew a Baravelle spiral on the clockwise copy of the wedge, you do not have to draw it again, because Baravelle spirals spin equally in both directions. Make a copy of the spiral, then shade a couple of spokes in counterclockwise direction.

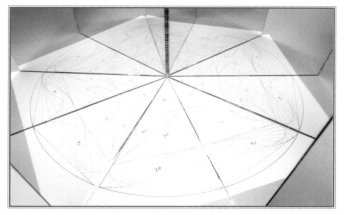

7 When you have filled each shape with a spiral, place the hinged mirrors along the sides of the wedge and watch the mandala bloom. This is a different mandala from the first one. However, since all of the spirals here spin in the same direction (counterclockwise), the flow forms are still all trunks.

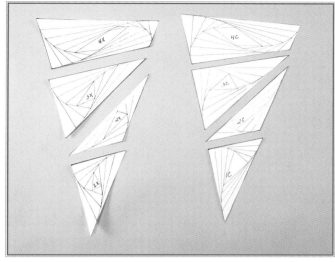

8 Make a few copies of each wedge with spirals in it. (Save the originals in the back of the page protector.)

Following the red shape lines, cut apart the spirals of one clockwise wedge and one counterclockwise wedge.

9 Put a loop of tape on the back of each spiral so they stick to the page protector and can be repositioned. Now you have a wedge puzzle.

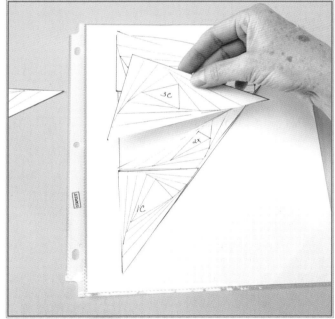

10 Using the wedge in the page protector as the skeleton, mix and match the clockwise and counterclockwise spirals in the wedge to make different mandalas.

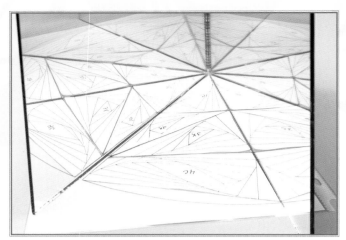

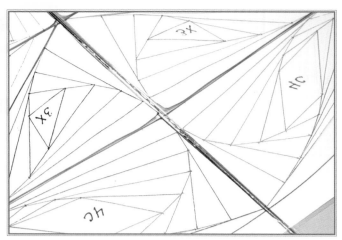

11 Each time you put together a different combination of counterclockwise and clockwise spirals, use the hinged mirrors to see how that version of the wedge will look as a complete mandala. Just like the mandalas you looked at before, each combination will be different. The photo here shows the wedge for *Crest of the Crane* on page 120.

12 As you explore your mandala designs, see how the spokes of the spirals connect to create flow forms. (We're going to explore flow forms more in the following pages.) Notice that when you combine clockwise and counterclockwise spirals you get a combination of fan and trunk flow forms in the mandala. Also, notice that every time you change the direction of a spiral in a shape, you change every flow form that connects to it. So, changing the direction of even one spiral can change the mandala completely.

Explore each mandala design in the mirrors by following the shapes and curves through the design with your finger or a pencil. You'll be tempted to start coloring in the designs that you see, so go ahead. You made extra copies of the spirals, so just cut another one if you mark this one.

Photograph the mandalas you like and photocopy the wedges to save them for reference (see page 156 for details on photocopying and photographing mandalas).

Here is Wedge 6 with one possible combination of clockwise and counterclockwise spirals. The full-circle illustration shows how it will look as a complete mandala. This will become *Crest of the Crane* on page 120.

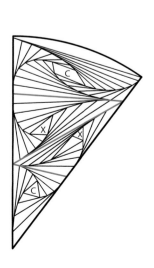

Q & A about Wedge Puzzles

What if a shape is too small to contain a spiral?

I call these little shapes "jewels" and they can be useful in several ways:
- Place a fussycut fabric detail in them, displaying a motif (this is where I get the name "jewel").
- Fill them with same fabric as adjoining spoke(s) to extend a spoke or connect two spokes.
- Subdivide them to help connect surrounding spirals. (I used this method in *Sultana* on page 144 to make the red spoke extend off the large spiral into the center.)

Do I have to put a spiral in every shape?

No. If you opt to leave a shape empty, treat is as you would a jewel, only larger. *That's the Way Love Is* (page 134) contains an empty shape.

How many possible mandalas are there in a single wedge?

The number of possible variations in any wedge is the number 2 with the number of shapes in the wedge as an exponent. So, for example, a wedge containing 4 shapes has 2^4 ($2 \times 2 \times 2 \times 2$) variations. That's 16 possible variations, as shown in the table below. (If the wedge is symmetrical, each combination on the right side of the table is the mirror image of the combination on the left side.)

But that's only counting mandalas made with a single wedge. If you use two or more wedges in compound symmetry (see page 30), the number of mandala possibilities in a group of wedges can go into the dozens. And the number of possible mandalas in a pie full of different wedges goes into the thousands.

What if a corner of a shape is too narrow and pointy?

Cut off the corner to create another side of the shape, then treat the cut-off corner like a jewel. I sometimes do this on the center point of the wedge; it keeps bulk out of the center by reducing seams or allows me to appliqué a center. It also creates a beautiful, thin ribbony spoke coming out of the center of the mandala. I did this in *Elizabeth* (page 128); *Crimes of Passion* (page 138) and *That's the Way Love Is* (page 134).

How do I photograph my potential mandalas?

To photograph a mandala, position a lamp directly over the mirrors so there are no shadows on the page. Position the camera at an angle to the mirrors where you can see the entire mandala as shown here. (For more about photographing mandalas, see page 156.)

SHAPE #			
1	2	3	4
C	C	C	C
X	C	C	C
C	X	C	C
C	C	X	C
C	C	C	X
C	X	X	C
X	X	C	C
C	X	C	X

SHAPE #			
1	2	3	4
X	X	X	X
C	X	X	X
X	C	X	X
X	X	C	X
X	X	X	C
X	C	C	X
C	C	X	X
X	C	X	C

FLOW FORMS

As you place spirals in your wedge skeleton, the spirals connect to create *flow forms*.

Most quilters are accustomed to seeing a design within a block, but flow forms happen between blocks when spirals connect. So, now you need to shift your perspective a bit. The straight-sided shapes are still there, and they are essential, because they are the spiral blocks that you sew. However, once you put spirals in the shapes, the curving flow forms become the most important aspect of the design and the straight sides of the shapes disappear (unless you deliberately emphasize them).

There are two types of flow forms: trunks and fans. Even though there are only two, they can vary widely depending on the proportions of the outer shape and the type of spiral you are drawing.

The outer shape primarily determines the proportions of the flow forms. A flow form coming off of a long side of a shape is compact, resembling wings, or the petals of a flower. A flow form coming off of a short side of a shape is thin and ribbony.

The type of spiral also affects the proportion of the flow form: Nesting and Pinwheel spirals usually have rather compact flow forms. Flow forms in Point-to-Point spirals, which are naturally more twirly, tend to curve more. And flow forms in Baravelle spirals, which are the most twirly, often stretch out so much that they look like ribbons.

The proportion of flow forms is another area of the design process where you need to let go of control and let the spirals themselves guide you. Later on, I'll show you a few ways to adjust the spirals a bit, but there's a limit to what you can control. (See Drawing Nesting Spirals, pages 61–65; Drawing Pinwheel Spirals, pages 67–70 and Advanced Spiral Techniques, pages 79–83.)

Trunk Flow Forms

Trunk flow forms appear when connecting spirals spin in the same direction—either both clockwise or both counterclockwise.

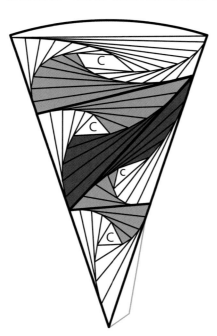 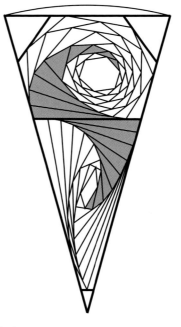

Above, Wedge 6 is filled with all clockwise spirals. Since all of the spirals spin in the same direction, all of the flow forms within the wedge (the shaded portions) are trunks. These are all Nesting Spirals, so the flow forms are compact, like wings.

In the wedge shown above (which is from *Elizabeth* on page 128), notice how the proportions of the trunk flow form change because of the differences in the shapes of the spirals. The top spiral is a Baravelle spiral, which is twistier than other types of spirals; the trunk flow form is therefore twistier as well. The proportions of a flow form—trunk or fan—can vary as infinitely as the shapes that contain them.

Fan Flow Forms

Fan flow forms appear where connecting spirals spin in opposite directions—one clockwise (C) and one counterclockwise (X). Notice in all the diagrams below how the proportions of the fans change because of differences in the shapes containing the spirals.

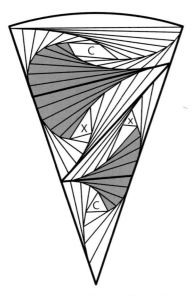

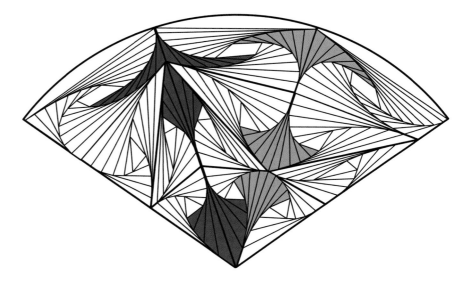

This diagram shows Wedge 6 filled with a combination of counterclockwise and clockwise spirals. The fan flow forms are shaded in gray. (This is the arrangement used for *Crest of the Crane* on page 120.)

Whenever you put two wedges side by side in mirror symmetry as shown above, the flow forms that cross from wedge to wedge will be fans, because the wedges and the connecting spirals are mirrored opposites of each other. (Learn More on Symmetry on pages 26–41.)

Flow Form Combinations

When you mix a variety of clockwise (C) and counterclockwise (X) spirals, you can get both trunk and fan flow forms.

In the diagram on the right, a mixture of clockwise and counterclockwise spirals results in a combination of fan flow forms (light gray) where opposite-direction spirals connect, and trunk flow forms (dark gray) where same-direction spirals connect.

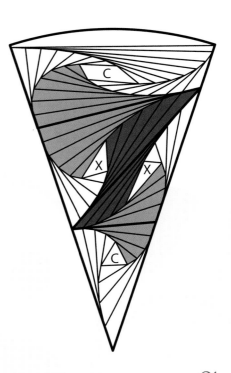

STEP 3: REPEATING THE WEDGE TO CREATE SYMMETRY

Finishing your spiral mandala design is simple: Repeat the wedge you have created to fill the pie. Follow the steps below for a complete mandala design.

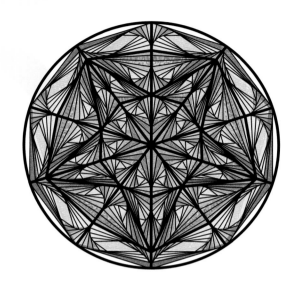

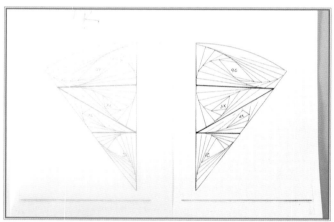

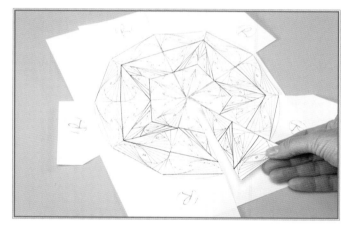

1 Make enough copies of your wedge to fill the entire mandala. Since you have been looking at your design with mirrors, the mandala you have created is in mirror symmetry. You'll need half the copies of the wedge in the original orientation and half in reverse. (See page 156 for detailed information about photocopying.)

If you like working in a large size, make copies of the full-size wedge puzzle. This will give you a complete mandala that is 20" across (diameter). If you want the whole mandala to fit on a single page (which is more convenient for experimenting with color placement), copy the wedge at 40% to take it from 10" to 4". Then, make full-size copies of the reduced wedge. This will give you a mandala with an 8" diameter that will fit on a single sheet of paper.

2 Join the copies of the wedges, alternating original and mirror orientations, to create the complete mandala. Make several copies of the full mandala drawing so you can experiment with different colorings. (See pages 42–55 for more information about color.)

Congratulations! You have just created your first spiral mandala quilt design. In the process, you mastered the basic techniques of dividing a wedge, drawing spirals, placing spirals in the shapes, creating flow forms and repeating the wedge in mirror symmetry.

Read the next two pages about backgrounds, borders and drafting on a computer, then skip ahead to Coloring a Spiral Mandala on page 42.

When you are ready to explore mandala design in more depth—including different types of symmetry and special wedge divisions—come back to More on Symmetry on pages 26–41.

Backgrounds and Borders

It's not too early to think about what will go around your mandala. Of course, you can use your mandala to create a round quilt; for example *Acts 2:3* (page 153) and *Tequila Sunrise* (page 31) are both round quilts. If you do want a square surrounding your mandala, here are two ways to do it.

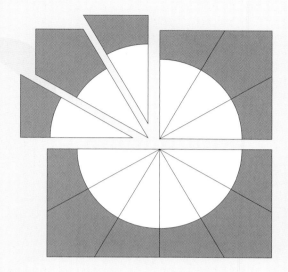

Pieced Background

Using this method, the background pieces are extensions of the wedge. Before joining the wedges, sew each background piece to its wedge. The background then goes together at the same time as the mandala. Background templates for most pies with up to 20 wedges are included on the enclosed CD. The templates will accommodate any wedge with a 10"–30" radius, and any background up to 60" square. Complete instructions for using them are printed on the templates. Instructions for joining the wedges and backgrounds are on page 111. Four of the six project quilts in this book have pieced backgrounds.

Appliqué Background

Appliquéing the mandala to the background is a good solution if you have a mandala with an irregular shape or if the background fabric has a specific direction, gradation or large pattern than you do not want to interrupt. It also does not require any advance planning.

After sewing the wedges together, sew a facing to the mandala to turn the edge smoothly. Appliqué the mandala to the background. Instructions are on pages 113–114. The mandala "pizza" shown below is appliquéd to the background.

Borders

Start thinking about borders now, too. A complicated mandala might benefit from a very simple border. On the other hand, piecing a border might help tie all of the elements in the quilt together. If you piece a border, consider including some spirals. Sometimes a border can be designed right into the mandala itself. In the case of the quilt shown here, the mandala is the border. Look closely at the borders of the quilts in this book to learn from what other quilters have done.

Pepperoni, Mushrooms, Double Cheese
Designed, pieced and quilted by Ruth Shadar
8 -wedge, mirror symmetry
39½" × 39½"

Fairest of Us All
Designed, pieced and quilted by Ruth Shadar
8 -wedge, mirror symmetry
24½" × 24½"

I've included instructions for creating a spiral mandala by hand because everyone has this technology at hand (yes, pun intended!). The process is slower than working on a computer, but if you choose you can view the time as an opportunity to relax and enjoy the meditative frame of mind that creating a mandala is meant to bring about. However, designing a mandala on a computer has many advantages, and here's some information that will enable you to draft your spiral mandala designs on a computer. Keep in mind, though, that the exploration and discovery of a design is still something best done by hand. There is simply no replacement for the freedom of a pencil and sheet of paper. Remember that the computer does not do the designing for you—it is only a tool. The ideas come from you, and even the greatest designers still sometimes sketch on napkins!

Electric Quilt

Designing spiral mandalas in EQ has advantages and disadvantages. Of the disadvantages, foremost is the fact that EQ requires that you draw within a square or rectangular block. And, since the number of lines you can draw within a single block is limited, it is impossible to draw a complete mandala within a single block unless it is very simple. However, it is possible to draft a single wedge, then use other tools in EQ to replicate it in a quilt layout; I have included instructions for doing that on the CD. (My abundant thanks to Betsy Vinegrad and Linda McGibbon for their insistence that this was possible and their persistence in figuring out how to do it.)

When drawing in EQ, you must connect every point precisely, or your drawing will not be accurate enough for coloring or sewing. Because of the interrelatedness of all the lines in a spiral, trying to adjust a mandala design in EQ can be a complicated process. For these reasons, I don't recommend EQ as a tool for exploring and discovering a design.

However, once you have decided on a design, you can draft that design in EQ (carefully and accurately!), then use EQ to easily experiment with fabric and color, and later, to calculate yardage and print out foundations and templates at any size you wish. These are big advantages.

In short, setting up a spiral mandala in EQ is not for beginners, but it can be done, and the advantages are worth the effort.

All of the templates for the projects in this book are provided in both .pdf and EQ formats.

Adobe Illustrator (and other graphic design programs)

I use Adobe Illustrator almost exclusively to draft my spiral mandala designs because I can draw them with no limitation to the form or the number of lines in the design, and making adjustments is quite simple. I do start exploring a design with paper and pencil, but once I have an idea, I draft a wedge in Illustrator, then the Flip and Rotate tools in Illustrator let me easily manipulate the wedge to fill in the pie in a couple of seconds. As in EQ, I can import fabrics into a swatch palette and color my designs using Illustrator's Live-Paint tool. Enlarging and printing foundations is quick and easy; either using the Scale tool or dragging to enlarge, I can create the size I want. I can also use the Text tool to label my templates in any way I wish, which is a huge plus. The only thing that Illustrator does not do for me is calculate yardage.

Other graphic design programs (like CorelDRAW) have similar functions. Look for them in the program that you work in. Learning to use these tools takes a bit of time, but is worth the effort.

Adobe Photoshop

Photoshop is not a program for drafting graphic designs. More recent versions of Photoshop have line-drawing capabilities similar to Illustrator, but the approach to handling graphics in Photoshop is still fundamentally different. I have Photoshop, and use it for many things, but not for drafting spiral mandalas.

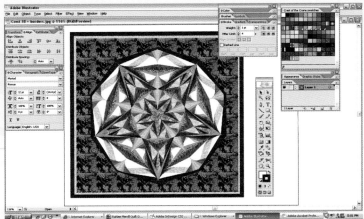

Star Light, Star Bright
Designed and pieced by Robin Armstead,
quilted by Joan Mork
10-wedge, mirror symmetry
72" × 82½"
Lots of contrasting colors combined with
mirror symmetry turn this mandala into a
kaleidoscopic starburst.

Angle of Rotation

Number of Wedges in the Pie	Angle of Each Wedge/Degree of Rotation
3	120°
4	90°
5	72°
6	60°
8	45°
9	40°
10	36°
12	30°
16	22.5°
18	20°
20	18°

More on Symmetry

For spiral mandalas, symmetry means repeating a wedge containing spirals around the pie to complete a circular design. Up until now, we have used mirrors to preview and design spiral mandalas with mirror symmetry. In addition to mirror symmetry, there are several other types of symmetry that you can use in your mandala design: *rotational symmetry, mixed symmetry* and *compound symmetry*. We'll explore these types of symmetry in Part 1 (pages 27–31).

For some types of symmetry, it is necessary to divide a wedge in a specific way. In Part 2 (pages 32–37), we'll learn about three types of wedge skeletons: *asymmetrical skeletons, symmetrical skeletons* and *asymmetrical skeletons with matching side nodes*.

You can also change the symmetry of a mandala by varying the direction of the spirals in some portions of a wedge. In Part 3 (pages 38–41), we'll look at spiral direction and how it affects symmetry in a mandala design.

I have tried to arrange the concepts here so that one builds on the next as much as possible, however, the ideas are by nature interwoven, so be prepared to flip around this section a bit.

About this Section

With what you have learned so far, you can successfully create a beautiful spiral mandala design.

The following section is like a graduate level course: It goes into deeper detail about how to use symmetry and wedge structure in a spiral mandala design. If you would like to stick to the basics for now, skip to Coloring a Spiral Mandala on page 42.

PART 1: TYPES OF SYMMETRY

MIRROR SYMMETRY

Up until now we have created mandalas with mirror symmetry. In mirror symmetry, the wedge and its reverse alternate around the pie.

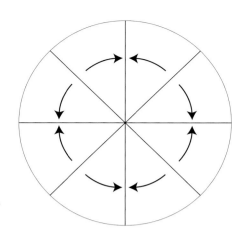

You can see a mandala in mirror symmetry by looking in hinged mirrors, or by making reverse copies of the original wedge. Flow forms that connect from wedge to wedge in mirror symmetry are always fans.

Best number of wedges for this type of symmetry:
Mirror symmetry works best in pies with an even number of wedges. However, mirrored symmetry can also be used in pies with odd numbers of wedges if the design contains other elements that fill in the odd wedge. One way to fill the odd wedge is to subdivide it in half and create another pair of smaller mirrored wedges.

Best kind of wedge to use for this type of symmetry:
Any wedge will work in mirror symmetry, because the sides of the wedges always match up with themselves.

Quilts in this book that use mirror symmetry:
Fairest of Us All, page 24
An Amazing Army of Frogs, page 27
A New Spin on the Snail's Trail, page 36
Cosmic Spin, page 43
Tropicale, page 45
Bliss, page 48
Mandalilies, page 49
Pieceful Sea, page 49
Flutter by the Garden, page 64
Reflections, page 70
Crest of the Crane, page 120
The Zebras Went Crazy, page 150
Blue Birds of Paradise, page 151
A Summer on Grant Island, page 152
There's a Rainbow In Here Somewhere. . ., page 153
The Empowerment of Women, page 154
Flow Blue, page 154
Nova 1038, page 155

An Amazing Army of Frogs
Designed, pieced and quilted by Susan Arnold
8-wedge, mirror symmetry
71" × 77"
Susan added interest to a simple mirrored design with a non-circular edge on the mandala that is echoed in the border. Frogs from the background peek through the centers of the spirals.

ROTATIONAL SYMMETRY

In rotational symmetry, a wedge is repeated around the pie in its original orientation, without being mirrored.

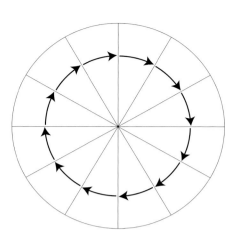

You cannot see a mandala in rotational symmetry by looking in mirrors. Instead, make copies of the wedge in the original orientation and place them side by side around the pie. Flow forms that connect from wedge to wedge in rotational symmetry can be trunks or fans depending on the directions of the adjoining spirals.

Best number of wedges for this type of symmetry:
Rotational symmetry works in pies with any number of wedges. It is particularly good for pies with odd numbers of wedges.

Best kind of wedge to use for this type of symmetry:
In rotational symmetry, side nodes need to match in order for flow forms to take shape between connecting wedges. You will need to use either a symmetrical wedge or an asymmetrical wedge with matching side nodes (see pages 32–37).

TIP

When you are preparing a wedge skeleton for rotational symmetry, before you start drawing spirals, make a copy and check both sides of the wedge to make sure the side nodes match.

Quilts in this book that use rotational symmetry:
Birds of Paradise, page 33
Up, Up and Away!, page 39
Magnetic Moments, page 46
Wind Power, page 61
Nocturno, page 67
That's The Way Love Is, page 134
Harmony, page 150

Majestic Mandalai
Designed and pieced by Rhonda Adams, quilted by Diane Anderson
12-wedge, rotational symmetry
47" × 47"
Rhonda began her mandala design with the idea of basing the structure on a Dresden Plate block. Trunks form between the wedges in the orange, purple and green areas. Take a close look at the award-winning quilting, especially in the borders.

28

MIXED SYMMETRY

In mixed symmetry, the same wedge is used in a combination of both mirror symmetry and rotational symmetry within the same pie. To look at it another way, you have both original and mirror-image copies of the wedge, but you don't alternate them (as you did in mirror symmetry). Instead, you group some "originals" and some "mirrors" together. There are many possible combinations within a pie.

To preview a mandala in mixed symmetry make several copies of the wedge in both original and reverse positions, then place them side-by-side around the pie in various combinations.

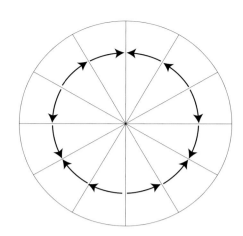

Best number of wedges for this type of symmetry:
Mixed symmetry works in pies with any number of wedges—it all depends on how you group the wedges.

Best kind of wedge to use for this type of symmetry:
Mandalas with mixed symmetry need wedges with side nodes that match up no matter which side is connecting with which. Use a symmetrical wedge or an asymmetrical wedge with matching side nodes (see pages 32–37).

Quilts in this book that use mixed symmetry:
Crimes of Passion, page 138

Heat Wave
Designed, pieced and quilted by
Ruth Shadar
12-wedge, mixed symmetry
50" × 58"
As Ruth arranged the 12 wedges of this quilt, she found more possibilities than the mirror symmetry she had originally planned.

The wedge is asymmetrical with matching side nodes, so it connects in both mirror and rotational symmetry (see page 37).

The images below show some of the other arrangements Ruth considered. The diagram above reflects her final choice.

COMPOUND SYMMETRY

A mandala doesn't have to use only one wedge. You can mix wedges divided differently, wedges of different widths and different types of wedges for a dramatic mandala design. All you have to do is pay attention to matching up the side nodes between the different wedges, particularly on the outside edges of the compound wedge. When you combine two or more different wedges and repeat them together around the mandala as a single unit, you are using compound symmetry. There are two types of compound symmetry: compound mirror symmetry and compound rotational symmetry.

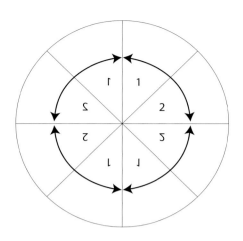

Compound mirror symmetry happens when a group of wedges is mirrored as a single unit to create repetition.

You can see a mandala in compound mirror symmetry by placing hinged mirrors along the outside edges of the group of wedges. Or, make reverse copies of the group of wedges.

Best number of wedges for this type of symmetry:
Compound mirror symmetry works best in pies with wedges in multiples of four; eight, twelve or sixteen wedges would work well, for example.

Best kind of wedge to use for this type of symmetry:
The individual wedges can be any of the three types of wedge. You do not need matching side nodes on the outside edges of a compound mirror group because the outer edges reflect and connect to themselves. The edge nodes on the adjoining edges within the compound wedge should match. Adjacent wedges in a Blind Man's Bluff are ideal for compound mirror symmetry because the inner side nodes already match.

Quilts in this book that use compound mirror symmetry:
Bliss, page 48 (2-wedge group)
Reflections, page 70 (3-wedge group)
Dancing Calla Lilies, page 75 (6-wedge group, half the mandala)
Elizabeth, page 128 (3-wedge group)

October Glory
Designed, pieced and quilted by Mary Reddington
8-wedge, compound mirror symmetry
55" × 55"
Each quarter of this mandala contains two different wedges that are mirrored as a group. Portions of this mandala are "blacked out" to create the scalloped edge and the white ribbon around the center area.

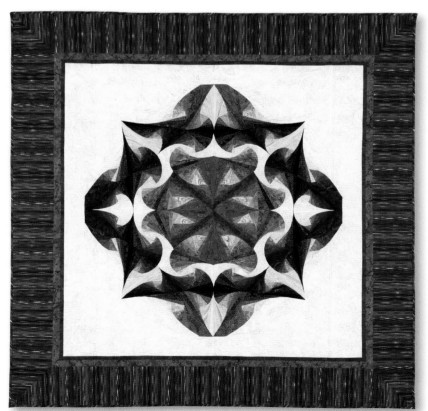

Compound rotational symmetry happens when the group of two or more wedges is rotated as a single unit to create repetition. (This is the most challenging type of symmetry to execute.)

To see a mandala in compound rotational symmetry, make copies of the group of wedges in its original orientation and place them side-by-side around the pie.

Best number of wedges for this type of symmetry:
Compound rotational symmetry works when the total number of wedges in the pie is a multiple of the number of wedges in the group. So, for example, a three-wedge group could work in a pie of six, nine, twelve or fifteen wedges. A two-wedge group would work in a pie with an even number of wedges.

Best kind of wedge to use for this type of symmetry:
The individual wedges can be any of the three types of wedge. However, the side nodes need to match on the outside edges of the group and on the adjoining edges within the group. Adjacent wedges in a Blind Man's Bluff are a good way to start, since the internal sides of the wedges already match. You'll still need to match up the side nodes on the outside edges of the group.

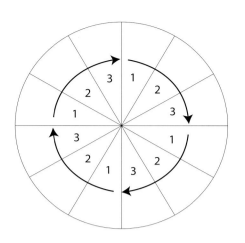

TIP

When you set up a wedge group for compound rotational symmetry, check the outside wedge skeletons against each other to make sure the side nodes match before you fill in the spirals.

Quilts in this book that use compound rotational symmetry:
Magnetic Moments, page 46
Easter Mandala, page 124
Rhythm of the Sun, page 151

Tequila Sunrise
Designed, pieced and quilted by Susan Ott
12-wedge, compound rotational symmetry
35" diameter
A group of three wedges makes up this mandala. Two are the same wedge in mirrored symmetry (the yellow "needle" up/down and across). The third contains the orange fan, which is the result of a well-managed T-joint (see T-Joints, page 41).

PART 2: TYPES OF WEDGES

There are three types of wedge skeletons: *asymmetrical wedge skeletons, symmetrical wedge skeletons* and *asymmetrical wedge skeletons with matching side nodes (AMSN)*. The important difference between them is whether or not the side nodes of the wedge match up with the side nodes of the adjacent wedge. Side nodes are the points where the dividing lines of a wedge meet the sides of the wedge; these are marked by red dots in the diagrams on this and the following pages.

If the side nodes of two wedges match, flow forms connect smoothly from wedge to wedge. If side nodes don't match, a straight line separates the wedges, interrupting the curving flow of your spiral mandala design and causing T-joints to form (see page 41).

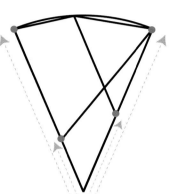

ASYMMETRICAL WEDGE

An asymmetrical wedge has side nodes that lie at different distances from the point of the wedge on each of its sides. This type of wedge may also have a different number of side nodes on each side.

Drawing an Asymmetrical Wedge

Most of the wedges that result from the Blind Man's Bluff technique are asymmetrical. To create an asymmetrical wedge skeleton without using the Blind Man's Bluff technique, divide the wedge in any way you wish. Lines can touch the sides and the outer curve of the wedge at any point. You can draw lines from one side of the wedge to the other, or try placing one or more dots in the middle of the wedge, then drawing lines from the dots to anywhere on the sides of the wedge. Just remember that all the shapes must have all corners pointing outward (see page 58), and try to avoid T-joints.

Setting an Asymmetrical Wedge in a Mandala

An asymmetrical wedge can connect to itself in mirrored symmetry. It can also connect to any other type of wedge as long as the side nodes match. Asymmetrical wedges do not work well when repeated in rotational symmetry because the side nodes won't match: The flow forms will not connect and straight lines will separate the wedges. T-joints will occur anywhere that side nodes do not match.

Since asymmetrical wedges work best in mirrored symmetry, they work best in mandalas with an even numbers of wedges. They can also be part of a group of wedges in compound symmetry.

Asymmetrical Wedges in Action

Mirrored symmetry   Rotational symmetry

The wedge shown above is an assymetrical wedge drawn using Blind Man's Bluff. In this wedge, there are two side nodes on each side at different distances from the point of the wedge. The dividing lines cross in the middle of the wedge, so there are no T-joints. (The Blind Man's Bluff method naturally avoids T-joints.) The shaded areas in these illustrations show connecting flow forms between wedges. The flow forms connect smoothly in mirrored symmetry. In rotational symmetry the flow forms don't connect because the side nodes don't match. Instead, straight lines separate the wedges and break up the curves of the design.

32

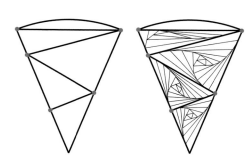

Mirrored symmetry   Rotational symmetry

The wedge shown here has three side nodes on the left and two side nodes on the right, all at different distances from the point of the wedge. The lines run from side to side, but do not cross in the middle of the wedge, so there are no T-joints.

The flow forms connect smoothly in mirrored symmetry but in rotational symmetry the flow forms don't connect because the side nodes don't match. Straight lines between the wedges break up the flow of the design.

Quilts in this book that use asymmetrical wedges:
Almost every quilt in this book that uses mirrored symmetry uses an asymmetrical wedge skeleton; some examples include:
An Amazing Army of Frogs, page 27
The Zebras Went Crazy, page 150
A Summer on Grant Island, page 152
There's a Rainbow In Here Somewhere. . .,
    page 153

Birds of Paradise
Designed, pieced and quilted by
Priscilla Roehm
10-wedge, rotational symmetry
26" diameter
Although this mandala features an asymmetrical wedge in rotational symmetry, careful color placement hides many of the straight lines between wedges. Within the wedges, color placement also creates some straight lines, so overall, straight lines become a strong element that unifies this spiral mandala design while hiding what might have been a design problem.

SYMMETRICAL WEDGE

A symmetrical wedge has side nodes that are the same distance from the point on both sides of the wedge. When folded down the middle, the two halves match exactly.

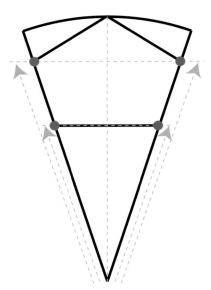

Drawing a Symmetrical Wedge

You have to plan a symmetrical wedge. To do so, place side nodes on both sides of the wedge at the same distance from the center point. The wedge can then be divided in two ways. The first is to divide the wedge symmetrically across its full width, so that all the shapes extend from side to side (Type 1); the wedge at right is a Type 1 symmetrical wedge. A second method divides part of the wedge down the middle; this part contains mirror-image shapes, while another part contains a single shape extending from side to side (Type 2).

Setting a Symmetrical Wedge in a Mandala

Symmetrical skeletons work alone in mirror, rotational and mixed symmetry. They can also combine with any other type of wedge in compound symmetry, as long as the side nodes match.

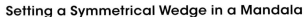

When is a symmetrical wedge not symmetrical?

When you put spirals in a symmetrical wedge, any spiral that crosses the center line gives it a single direction. The filled wedge is no longer symmetrical and it behaves like an AMSN wedge (see page 37). So, it is often helpful to think of a symmetrical wedge as only a symmetrical skeleton; the skeleton is symmetrical for purposes of connecting with other wedges, no matter which direction the spirals spin.

Symmetrical Wedges in Action

Type 1: This symmetrical skeleton is divided across the wedge, so all the spirals extend from side to side. The shaded areas show connecting flow forms between wedges in both mirror and rotational symmetry.

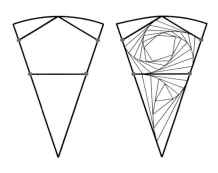

Quilts in this book that use Type 1 symmetrical wedges:
Majestic Mandalai, page 28
Elizabeth, page 128
Renaissance Dreams, page 152

Mirrored symmetry

Rotational symmetry

Type 2: In this type of symmetrical wedge, part of the wedge is divided in half to create mirror-image shapes, while another part of the wedge contains a single symmetrical shape that crosses the center line. (This shape may or may not extend all the way across the wedge.) The spirals in the mirror-image shapes may spin in opposite (mirror) directions to form a fan (top row of diagrams) or in the same direction to form a trunk (bottom row of diagrams). The spiral that spans the center line always has a single direction, and because of this the filled wedge is never perfectly symmetrical.

If you set any Type 2 symmetrical wedge in mirror symmetry, the entire mandala will have mirror symmetry (as demonstrated by the mandala at left in the top and bottom rows). But if you set it in rotational symmetry, the mandala can have either a combination of rotational and mirror symmetry (top row, far right) or all rotational symmetry (bottom row, far right), depending on the directions of the spirals in the mirror-image shapes.

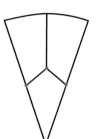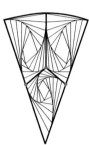

Type 2 wedge with mirrored spirals in mirror-image shapes at top

Set in mirrored symmetry, the wedge creates a mandala with mirror symmetry.

Even set in rotational symmetry, this wedge creates a mandala with both rotational and mirror symmetry, because the wedge contains mirrored spirals.

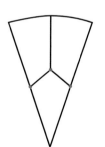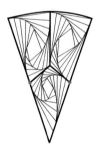

Type 2 wedge with same-direction spirals in mirror-image shapes at top

Set in mirrored symmetry, the wedge creates a mandala with mirror symmetry.

Set in rotational symmetry, this wedge creates a mandala with all rotational symmetry, because there is no mirror symmetry within the wedge.

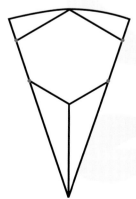

Here is another version of a Type 2 symmetrical wedge. The large, rounded central shape is excellent for holding a Baravelle or Point-to-Point spiral. Wedges similar to this one are used in the "Type 2" quilts listed here.

Quilts in this book that use Type 2 symmetrical wedges:
Cosmic Spin, page 43
Magnetic Moments, page 46
Blueberry Swirl Sundae, page 71
Easter Mandala, page 124 (Lily wedge)
Sultana, page 144
I Think I'm Losing My Marbles, page 155

While it may seem that a third method of creating a symmetrical wedge would be to split the wedge all the way down the middle and then divide each side symmetrically, this in fact creates a mirrored pair of two asymmetrical wedge skeletons, not a single symmetrical wedge.

If mirrored spirals are set in this group, the result is a mirrored pair of asymmetrical wedges. (Ironically, the only way to create a perfectly symmetrical wedge filled with spirals is with asymmetrical wedges!) However, if spirals of various directions are set in the group this would create two different asymmetrical wedges joined in a compound symmetry group—which is not symmetrical.

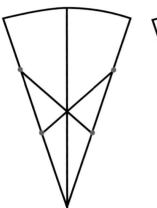

Wedge skeleton with center dividing line

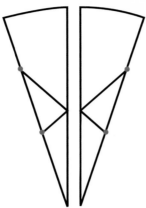

Two narrow asymmetrical wedge skeletons

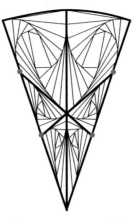

Two narrow asymmetrical wedge skeletons set with mirrored spirals

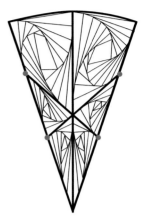

Two narrow asymmetrical wedge skeletons set with spirals of various directions

A New Spin on the Snail's Trail
Designed, pieced and quilted by
Anita Mester
6-wedge, mirror symmetry
51½" × 57½"
In this quilt Anita achieved the nearly impossible—a symmetrical wedge with perfect internal symmetry—by placing solid fabrics (not spirals) in all the shapes that cross the center line of the wedge. Although the design is hexagonal, all of the spirals in it are traditional square Snail's Trail blocks, or what I call square Baravelle spirals.

ASYMMETRICAL WEDGE WITH MATCHING SIDE NODES

An asymmetrical wedge with matching side nodes (AMSN wedge) has side nodes that are the same distance from the point on both sides of the wedge, but its internal skeleton is asymmetrical. If it is folded down the middle, the side nodes match, but the internal shapes do not.

Drawing an AMSN Wedge

Place side nodes on both sides of the wedge at the same distance from the point. You can also place nodes on the outer edge. You must have the same number of side nodes on each side. Divide the wedge asymmetrically, with lines meeting the sides of the wedge only at the side nodes. Try placing one or more dots in the middle of the wedge, then draw connecting lines from the side nodes to the dot.

Setting an AMSN Wedge in a Mandala

AMSN wedges connect to themselves in mirror symmetry, rotational symmetry and mixed symmetry. They can also connect to any other type of wedge in compound symmetry, as long as the side nodes match.

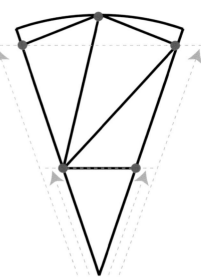

In an AMSN wedge, the side nodes on each side of the wedge are the same distance from the point of the wedge, so the flow forms connect smoothly from wedge to wedge in both mirror symmetry and rotational symmetry. The shaded areas in the illustrations below show connecting flow forms between wedges.

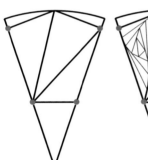   

Mirrored symmetry   Rotational symmetry

TIP

You can "plan" a Blind Man's Bluff to create an AMSN wedge by setting equidistant side nodes on some wedges, then drawing lines through them across the pie. Wedges adjacent to the "planned" wedges will most often be asymmetrical, but they will connect perfectly to the AMSN wedge.

This is the AMSN wedge used in *Heat Wave* (page 29). Look carefully at the finished quilt and variations to see how the matching side nodes allow the arrangement of the wedges to change.

Quilts in this book that use AMSN wedges:

Heat Wave, page 29
That's the Way Love Is, page 134
Crimes of Passion, page 138

PART 3: SPIRAL DIRECTION

So far we have talked about symmetry in terms of setting up the structure of the skeleton and setting the complete wedge in mirror or rotational symmetry. However, there is one more level where symmetry can vary: the direction of the spirals within the skeleton.

Remember that spirals are directional—they spin either clockwise or counterclockwise. If you start with identical wedge skeletons, but have the spirals going in different directions within them, the filled wedges are different. This can lead to all kinds of design fun. For example, in both *Cosmic Spin* (page 43) and *Dancing Calla Lilies* (page 75), most of the mandala is in mirror symmetry, but changing the direction of one spiral in a wedge sets up a different pattern of symmetry in the ribbon around the outside of the design. You can recognize a mandala with changes in spiral direction because of this characteristic; as you look from the center of the mandala toward the edge, some parts of the repeated wedges are in mirror symmetry and other parts are in rotational symmetry.

Bolero
Designed and pieced by Deb Sorem, quilted by Janet Fogg
10-wedge, mirror symmetry with changing spiral direction
38" × 40"
The wedge skeleton of this mandala is set in mirror symmetry, but the direction of one spiral in every other wedge is reversed, so the green and aqua spirals are set in rotational symmetry.

Quilts in this book that feature changes in spiral direction:
Cosmic Spin, page 43
Dancing Calla Lilies, page 75
Elizabeth, page 128
Rhythm of the Sun, page 151
Renaissance Dreams, page 152

A few last thoughts about designing a mandala

Breaking out of the wedge ... or the circle

While wedges are a beautiful and convenient way to structure a mandala, they are not the only way. If you want to divide the circle along other lines, go ahead. For that matter, you don't have to use a circle either!

Up, Up and Away!
Designed, pieced and quilted by Susan Wood
12-sided with non-wedge divisions
49" × 49"
This mandala is built in a round 12-sided shape, but the sections are not wedges with points at the center.

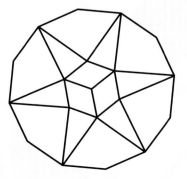

Quilts in this book that are not based on a wedge or a circle:
Fireball, page 40 (hexagon with non-wedge divisions)
Supernova, page 40 (irregular pentagon)
Reflections, page 70 (oval)
A Summer on Grant Island, page 152 (square)

39

Spiral Centers

Placing a spiral at the center of a mandala gives it an interesting focal point and can force you to break out of a purely wedge-based structure. From a technical standpoint, placing a spiral at the center of a mandala is one way to avoid joining many narrow pointed seams at the center of a mandala.

Supernova
Designed and pieced by Dottie Lankard, quilted by Cotie Campbell
10-wedge, mirror symmetry
50" × 41"
A 10-sided Baravelle spiral at the center of this quilt connects into five irregularly shaped wedges, each containing two Nesting spirals. Dottie's goal was to make a mandala that had only a few spirals, yet was still a strong, unique design. (Then she spent the time she saved beading it!)

Fireball
Designed and pieced by Amy Dawdy
65" × 65"
An 8-sided point-to-point spiral at the center of this mandala explodes into a hexagonal design that is not based on a wedge, and combines both mirror and rotational symmetry.

Watch Out for T-joints

Sometimes when you divide a wedge you'll end up with the corners of two shapes meeting in the middle of a side of another shape; I call this a T-joint. T-joints almost always result in straight lines that interrupt the curves of the flow forms. T-joints can happen inside a wedge, and they always happen between wedges when the side nodes don't match. T-joints will not happen between wedges when the side nodes do match.

I usually try to avoid or eliminate T-joints. The Blind Man's Bluff method of dividing wedges never creates T-joints, so using that technique is one easy way to avoid them. If you use another method to divide a wedge, in order to avoid T-joints, don't start or end a line in the middle of another line—always draw a new line across another line to the corner of a shape or the side of the wedge.

If you do leave a T-joint in your design, the flow forms around a T-joint usually take one of three forms—a double hook, a fork or a fan—depending on the direction the spirals are spinning. Of the three, the fan is the only real flow form, and looks best with other flow forms. Whatever shape a T-joint takes, try to color it in a way that integrates it elegantly into your design.

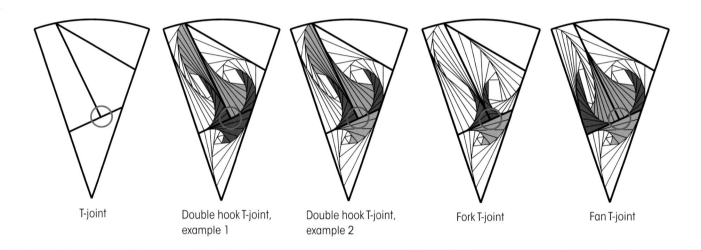

| T-joint | Double hook T-joint, example 1 | Double hook T-joint, example 2 | Fork T-joint | Fan T-joint |

Solutions for T-joints:

If a T-joint is a fan, the shapes around it can be colored so as to avoid a straight line against it.

To eliminate a T-joint, divide and bend the straight line to create a corner where the other shapes meet. This adds a side to one shape, adding a spoke to that spiral. Redraw both the spiral with the new spoke and the spiral with the adjusted shape.

Another option is to extend the center line across the straight line to create a new shape, which is then filled with a spiral. Try different directions in all the spirals to see what makes the best new arrangement.

These last two solutions involve moving a side node, so you might also need to readjust adjacent wedges. It's best to make these adjustments to the skeleton before drawing in any spirals.

Fan T-joint colored to avoid straight lines

T-joint eliminated by dividing and bending the straight line

T-joint eliminated by extending the center line

41

Coloring a Spiral Mandala

FINDING THE DESIGN

The first step in coloring your mandala is to find the forms you want to emphasize. Make several copies of the line drawing of your mandala. Beginning with just a pencil, shade in different areas. Let your pencil wander, following the curves and flow of the design. As you move on to color (see page 50), continue to be aware of how value can affect the structure and form of your mandala design.

As you explore, choose which forms will be positive space (the design you want to emphasize) and which areas will be negative space (the background). Watch how value—light and dark—make some areas prominent and others disappear. Look at the quilts throughout this book and observe how the placement of light and dark values forms the visible design. (Photocopying them in black and white will help you better see value and structure.)

The main design elements in a spiral mandala are the curving flow forms, so let these guide the structure of your design. The next few pages will show you several ways to shade and color flow forms: solid, gradation, split, variegated, linked and flowunders.

Here are four different shadings of the mandala skeleton used in *Crest of the Crane* (page 120). Simply changing the placement of light and dark changes the design significantly. A variety of colored examples of this mandala can be found on page 54.

SOLID FLOW FORMS

A solid spoke or flow form has all its triangles filled with the same fabric. For this purpose, solid refers to using a single fabric—the fabric can be a solid color or a pattern. In a solid flow form, all the triangles of the same fabric merge together to create a single, curving form.

Solid coloring is usually the best choice for thin spokes—the single fabric holds them together visually over the distance, defining them clearly as they bump up against other fabrics.

In thicker spokes, using a single fabric creates a solid form that may anchor and calm busier elements of the design, or might be too heavy in relation to other parts of the design. It's up to you to make the creative judgment call.

Another way to use solid flow forms in a mandala design is to black-out a section. When you place the background fabric in some areas of the mandala, these areas "disappear" leaving "open" areas in the design. (In art terms, this is "negative space.") Blacking out areas around the outside of a mandala gives it a scalloped edge.

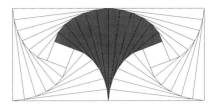

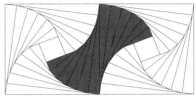

In a line drawing you can see all of the beautiful triangles in a spiral, but with the same fabric in all of them, the triangles merge into a single, solid shape. To see separate triangles, use one of the coloring methods on the next few pages.

Cosmic Spin
Designed and pieced by Betsy Vinegrad, quilted by Gwen Baggett
8-wedge, mirror symmetry
59½" × 59½"
All the flow forms in this mandala are colored solid; some are "blacked out" with background fabric to set off the white ribbon and outer blue/green ring. A Type 2 symmetrical wedge (see page 35) creates 8-wedge mirrored symmetry in the white ribbon and red hearts and 16-wedge symmetry everywhere else.

Quilts in this book that use solid flow forms:

Quilts in this book that use blacked-out areas in the mandala:

GRADATION FLOW FORMS

In a gradation, a gradual change from light to dark or from color to color occurs as each adjacent triangle of a spoke or flow form is filled with a different fabric. When a gradation is used, the flow form holds together visually and the curves are visible, plus you get to see all those wonderful pieced triangles!

Gradations also create the illusion of depth. To get a three-dimensional effect, place darker colors where you want distance or depth and lighter colors where you want closeness or height.

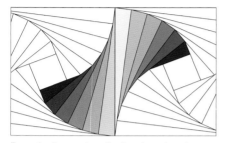 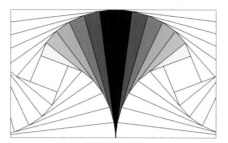 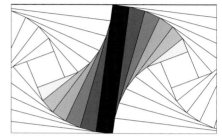

To make the center of a flow form bend toward you, place lights in the center and go darker at the edges.

To make the center of a flow form bend away from you, place darker areas at the center and lighter areas at the edges.

Avoid putting the same fabric in the two connecting triangles of a trunk flow form. This creates a horizontal bar across the middle of the flow form that can interrupt a curving design.

Three Kinds of Gradations

Value Gradation: The value of the same color changes from dark to light or vice versa.

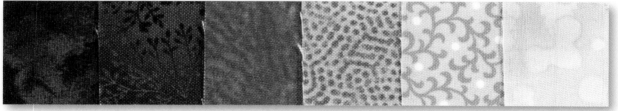

Inversion Gradation: A two-color combination switches to its opposite—this one goes purple/green to green/purple.

Color-to-Color Gradation: Blend one or more colors to completely different colors. Introduce the new color in the middle of the gradation, then phase out one or more of the colors you began with.

The key to smooth transitions from color to color in either an inversion or color-to-color gradation is a middle fabric that has equal proportions of both the old and the new colors.

44

Spiraling Out of the Box
Designed, pieced and quilted by
Martha Flanagan
12-sided outer shape divided into 4 wedges,
mirror symmetry, rectangular center
14⅝" diameter
There are 5 or more steps of gradation in
every spoke of every spiral in this design. This
miniature quilt contains over 600 pieces.

Glowing Gradations

You can use gradations to make
your mandala appear as though
light is shining through it. Use a
light color at the center of the
spiral, then graduate values in
the spokes, starting light near the
center and going darker as you
move out. You can see this effect in
Sultana, page 144.

Tropicale
Designed, pieced and quilted by Mary Reddington
8-wedge, mirror symmetry
43" × 43"
Gorgeous 8-step gradations throughout this quilt make the colors seem to flow
like water. Placing the light part of the aqua gradation around the orange star at
the center makes the star seem to glow.

**Quilts in this book that use gradation flow
forms:**
About half the quilts in this book use gradation
in at least part of the mandala design. Take a tour
through the book and look closely at how each
quilt uses gradation in its own unique way. A few
of the best examples of gradation flow
forms include:
An Amazing Army of Frogs, page 27
Magnetic Moments, page 46
Flutter by the Garden, page 64
There's a Rainbow In Here Somewhere...,
    page 153

LINKED FLOW FORMS

One of the most beautiful ways to color flow forms is to link them through more than one spiral, creating ribbons. This is simple to do—color two spokes on opposite sides of a spiral in the same color, then fill the center with the same color to link them. Continue the color through the flow form into the next spiral, which you color the same way. Linked flow forms look three-dimensional when combined with gradation.

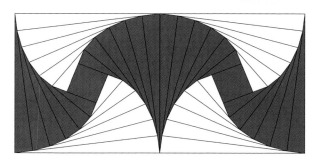 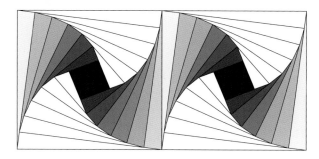

To link flow forms, continue the color or gradation of a flow form through the center of its spiral and into another flow form on the other side.

Quilts in this book that use linked flow forms:
October Glory, page 30 (white ring around center)
Cosmic Spin, page 43 (white ribbon)
Mandalilies, page 49 (green/gold border)
Dancing Calla Lilies, page 75 (black ribbon)
That's the Way Love Is, page 134 (blue around edge)
Crimes of Passion, page 138 (red and black around edge)
There's a Rainbow in Here Somewhere . . ., page 153 (black in outer edge)

Magnetic Moments
Designed, pieced and quilted by Georgianne Kandler
8-wedge, compound rotational symmetry
48" × 48"
This mandala uses linked flow forms to create the green ribbon border. The light-dark gradation gives makes the ribbon appear to twist over and under.

FLOWUNDERS

When I look at a mandala design, I often see spokes and flow forms passing over and under one another. I call these areas flowunders. Flowunders give the impression that a mandala has several layers and help to tie a design together by making a color or gradation travel from one part of a design to reappear in another.

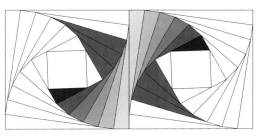

To create a flowunder, watch for places where triangles in one spiral align with triangles in another spiral on opposite sides of a flow form. Make the triangles on both sides the same color or gradation to create the flowunder. Be aware of this as you draft your foundations so you can align the triangles (see page 88). You can also use value to help emphasize the appearance of layers: Place lighter values in areas that pass over and darker values in areas that pass under. (This is not a hard-and-fast rule, but it is helpful to keep in mind as you experiment.)

Flowunders can be created with or without gradations, but gradations enhance the illusion of a three-dimensional design. Place the darker pieces in a gradation where the flow form passes under—this creates the look of a shadow falling from the area "above" onto the area "below."

Sultana
Designed and pieced by RaNae Merrill, quilted by Diane Anderson
54½" × 54½"
This mandala includes several flowunders (pattern, page 144).

In the photo above, the light green spoke flows under the red spoke, the gold fan flows under the light green spoke and the green gradation flows under the gold fan.

Here, the gold fans at the center (detail above) flow under the large spirals to reappear in the outer border. A green gradation flows under this gold fan as at the center.

47

SPLIT FLOW FORMS

A split flow form is created when value changes abruptly within the flow form, usually at the connection between two spirals. A split can occur in either a solid or gradation flow form. The light/dark contrast at the split creates a straight line that highlights the straight-sided outer shape of a spiral, or a straight line within a spiral, rather than curving spokes and flow forms. If you use many split flow forms, they can obscure most of the curves in the design.

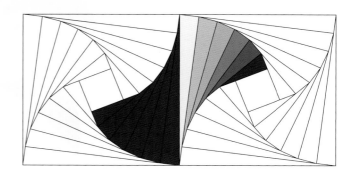

Quilts in this book that use split flow forms:
Majestic Mandalai, page 28
Tequila Sunrise, page 31
Flutter by the Garden, page 64
Nocturno, page 67
A Summer on Grant Island, page 152
There's a Rainbow in Here Somewhere . . ., page 153 (purple star at center)

Bliss
Designed and pieced by Rhonda Adams, quilted by Karen Overton
16-wedge, compound mirror symmetry
45" × 45"
The split flow forms in Rhonda's mandala frame other flow forms colored in gradations.

48

VARIEGATED FLOW FORMS

A variegated flow form has different colors and values in different triangles of the same spoke. This often creates a kaleidoscopic effect in which curves and flow forms practically disappear. To take another approach, selectively coloring some of the triangles in a spiral lets you highlight a non-spiral design.

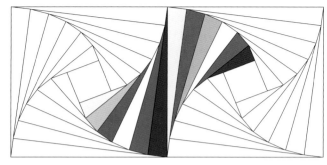

Pieceful Sea
Designed, pieced and quilted by
Debra Nance
10-wedge, mirror symmetry
32" × 32"
A variety of contrasting fabrics are placed within the flow forms of this mandala. This fractures their continuity, resulting in a kaleidoscopic design.

Mandalilies
Designed, pieced and quilted by Linda Cooper
8-wedge, mirror symmetry
47" × 47"
Linda loves flowers, so even in her mandala she found a way to design them. By carefully selecting certain triangles in the spirals, she made lilies appear in both the central mandala and the border.

Quilts in this book that use variegated flow forms or selective coloring:

CHOOSING COLOR AND FABRIC

Now you have the form and structure of your design worked out. If you haven't already done so, it's time to choose your color scheme. Then, choose fabrics that will carry out the color scheme and add pattern to the design.

COLOR SCHEME

Begin by choosing three or four colors for your basic color scheme. Some ways to come up with a color scheme are:

- Find a fabric you like and build a color scheme from that.

- Take a trip to your local paint store to browse paint swatches. Go with a friend and challenge each other to come up with interesting combinations.

- Look at pictures in design or travel magazines. Pay close attention to the colors in different environments: What impressions do they bring to mind? What feelings do they evoke?

- Give copies of your mandala drawing to friends or family members—including children—and ask them to color in the design. Chances are, they'll see the design in ways and in colors that never occurred to you at all, giving you a fresh perspective on both color and design.

- Choose colors that you (or the quilt recipient) already have in your home decor.

Besides the actual colors themselves, pay attention to proportion—how much of each color you put into the design. A lot of black with a little orange, for example, is much different than a lot of orange with a little black!

Notice in this detail shot of *Elizabeth* (page 128) the strong contrast between the light gold background and the center, which makes the design stand out. Also, placing a darker shade of blue next to the gold "rays" in the center adds depth to the design by creating a "shadow" beneath this edge.

VALUE

When choosing colors, you need a mix of light, medium and dark values.

After you've chosen your colors, add some lighter and darker values of each color. If you plan to use gradations, you'll need several different values. Even if you don't plan to use gradations, having just two shades of at least one of your colors can help give depth to a design.

I can't stress enough how important value is in any quilt design: Contrasting values are the only way we can see the structure of a design. Place contrasting values in adjacent spokes or flow forms to separate and define them clearly. Place similar values within a spoke or flow form, or in any other area you want to hold together visually.

TIP

To see value clearly, photocopy, photograph or scan your fabrics in black and white. A ruby beholder (it's basically a piece of red plastic) will also reduce colors to only their value. If nothing else, look at a group of fabrics with your eyes squinted nearly shut to compare value more easily.

PATTERN

When I select fabrics for a mandala, I combine three types of fabrics: foundation fabrics, energy fabrics and jewelry fabrics. Each type of fabric plays an important role in bringing the design to life.

Foundation fabrics

Foundation fabrics are solids, small tone-on-tone prints and textures. These are the backbone of your design, setting the color palette and defining the shapes. You can use foundation fabrics anywhere in a mandala. Since the patterns are tiny and non-directional, they fit in any size piece of the design. They are the best choice for narrow spokes and flow forms. In gradations, they create smooth, subtle shifts from value to value. However, an entire mandala in these well-behaved fabrics can be bit dull, so it's a good idea to mix in some energy fabrics.

Green foundation fabrics from *Crest of the Crane* on page 120

Energy fabrics

Energy fabrics have medium-sized, multicolored patterns. They add sparkle and vitality to any design. For spirals, select non-directional patterns that are small enough to see in the narrow triangles. You may need to fussy-cut small pieces to achieve a consistent color and/or texture across an entire area. Use energy fabrics in solid flow forms that are large enough to show the pattern. Work them into gradations to add texture or to change from one color to another.

Green energy fabrics from *Crest of the Crane*

Jewelry fabrics

Jewelry fabrics are large-scale prints. They are like a lapel pin on a business suit or a necklace with a dress; they create focal points in your design. Use jewelry fabrics in the centers of spirals and the center of the mandala; these are ideal places to feature a fussy-cut motif. If you are working in mirror symmetry, look for symmetrical prints that you can place in reflection where spirals join. Appliqué a fussy-cut detail over a finished mandala. Backgrounds and borders are good places to show off a large-scale pattern. Pick up bits of the same fabric within the mandala (even if it's really subtle) to create unity between the mandala design and the border.

The jewelry fabric used for the appliqués and background in *Crest of the Crane*

Repetition

Use each fabric in at least two places in the overall design—don't "orphan" a fabric. Repeating fabrics helps the viewer's eye move across the design to see symmetry. The repetition can be prominent or subtle. For example, try picking up a little bit of the border fabric within a gradation where it's hardly even seen; even this little bit is caught by our mind's eye and ties these areas together.

TIP

Place foundation fabrics alongside energy fabrics for the contrast necessary to contain and define a shape.

51

Turning a Color Scheme into Fabric Choices

To help you understand the process of choosing color and fabric, I'm going to walk you through how I selected fabrics for *Crest of the Crane* (pattern, page 120).

The color scheme came from the jewelry fabric at right. (Each crane is approximately 10" wide, and the flowers are life-size.) It included blue, green, pink, gold and white.

Once I choose my color scheme, I pull every fabric in my stash that I think might fit. I do the same thing at the fabric store—thankfully, they are very patient when I start stacking up bolt after bolt of fabric on the table!

1 I begin by sorting the fabrics into groups of the same color:

2 Next, I sort each color group into foundation fabrics, energy fabrics and jewelry fabrics. I usually mix these up again in gradations, but this step lets the fabrics influence the design. Often this is when I "fall in love" with a fabric or group of fabrics that absolutely must go in the design, and all my other fabric choices revolve around that fabric.

At each step along the way, I eliminate fabrics that are the wrong shade or have personalities that don't work with the group.

Foundation Fabrics

Energy Fabrics

Jewelry Fabrics

3 Then, I arrange each color group into gradations from dark to light. There are often several possible gradations in each color group depending on which fabrics I include and how many steps are in the gradation. As I sort and experiment, I check the areas of the design where I plan to place a gradation to see how many steps of value change I have and note where I might need additional shades of a fabric for a gradation. (Since I haven't drafted the final foundations yet, I also have the option of creating the number of steps I want based on the fabric I have.)

4 My last step is auditioning the fabrics in the mandala. Since I already did a preliminary plan of the value and color placement, I have a pretty good idea of where the fabrics will go in the design, but I still try other variations. Often, working with the fabrics prompts new ideas—sometimes I even change fabrics. Here are a few of the ideas I tried for *Crest of the Crane.*

Auditioning Fabrics on the Computer

One of the great advantages of designing on a computer is the ability to quickly and easily change color. You can load fabric swatches into the program so you can place them in the design to see how the fabrics will actually look. It takes some time and effort to set up the design and scan the swatches, but ultimately it's worth the ease of auditioning fabrics. (And, later, printing templates at any size you want.) Keep in mind, however, that every computer screen, scanner and printer is different in how it represents color, so colors you view on the screen or in print are usually not completely accurate.

Many quilters use Electric Quilt (EQ) for this. I use either EQ or Illustrator, depending on the project.

Instructions for scanning and importing swatches in EQ5 can be found on pages 158 and 164 of the *EQ5 Design Cookbook.* For EQ6 instructions, see pages 138–139 of the *EQ6 User Manual.*

For instructions on coloring and setting up an entire mandala in EQ, refer to the file entitled Creating Mandalas in EQ on the CD that came with this book.

Auditioning Fabrics "In Person"

To audition fabrics "in person," cut pieces of fabric and place them in a mock-up of your wedge. If you have a limited amount of fabric, make color photocopies of the fabric and cut the photocopy into pieces to fill your wedge. If you want to see the full mandala with the fabrics, use the mirrors or photocopy the wedge with the fabrics. If you are working in mirror symmetry, this is one time when being able to photocopy in mirror image is really helpful, as photocopying onto translucent paper and flipping it over won't show you fabric colors as they will appear in the quilt. (See page 156 for photocopying guidelines.)

TIP

If a fabric is currently in production, the fabric company or a store online will likely have a swatch on their Web site that you can download to your computer and then import into your design program, saving you the time and effort of scanning it.

When I originally chose the fabrics for *Crest of the Crane*, I selected mostly solids and textures and set aside most of the energy fabrics, ruling them out as too busy. But when I put all those foundation fabrics together, something was lacking. I started switching out foundation fabrics, replacing them with energy fabrics. In the end, I chose mostly energy fabrics.

Also, I realized that many of the variations shown here were too busy or complicated, so I started eliminating fabrics and details. For example, I included a black fabric in my original choices, but eliminated it because it was too heavy. Getting a design just right often involves removing distractions to allow the best parts to shine through.

Here are my final fabric choices for *Crest of the Crane*. Look closely at the finished quilt to see where each fabric is placed and observe the effect that it has on the overall design. Study the quilts throughout this book with the same attention to see how other quilters have used color, value and pattern in their quilts.

Ultimately, choosing the right fabrics comes down to what you like and what accomplishes the goal of your design. As your understanding of color, value and pattern grows, you will become better and better at making interesting, successful fabric choices for all your quilts.

Crest of the Crane
10-wedge, mirrored symmetry
Pattern, pages 120–123

CHAPTER TWO

Preparing Foundations and Sewing Your Spiral Mandala Quilt

Congratulations—you have completed a beautiful spiral mandala design!

This new chapter will take you through the entire process of turning your design into a finished quilt.

First, I'll help you learn to draw spirals. If you have already worked through the first portion of the book, you have used the basic spiral-drawing techniques to create a wedge puzzle. As in Chapter 1, this section presents the basics first, then adds some more advanced techniques. Even if you are already familiar with spirals, chances are you'll still find something new here, and you will likely refer to both the basic and more advanced drawing instructions as you draft your foundations.

Next, we'll work step by step through the process of drafting and preparing the templates and foundations you will need to sew your mandala. Spirals are foundation pieced (or paper-pieced, as some people call it). If foundation piecing is new to you, don't worry—it's not complicated. If you are an experienced foundation piecer, you might find some techniques here that will make foundation piecing easier than ever.

Last, I'll help you bring your mandala to life as you sew the individual spirals, then assemble them into wedges, a mandala and a finished quilt. If you can sew a Log Cabin block, you can sew a spiral. And if you thought your design was beautiful on paper, wait until you see it in fabric!

Drawing Spirals

ABOUT SPIRALS

Spirals are the essential building blocks of a spiral mandala design: You place a spiral in each shape within the wedge. There are four types of spirals: Nesting, Baravelle, Point-to-Point and Pinwheel. Draw each type of spiral and get comfortable with the terms used to talk about spirals. Even if you have drawn spirals before, it's a good idea to review and refresh what you know.

SHAPES FOR SPIRALS

For a spiral mandala, start with a wedge and divide it into shapes. You can draw a spiral in any shape, as long as the corners all point outward and the sides are straight. There are several different kinds of shapes that may appear in your wedge. A shape that has all sides the same length is *equilateral*. A shape that can be folded equally in half (it can have all sides the same length, or not) is *symmetrical*. A shape that has all different sides and corner angles is irregular. Most of the shapes in your wedges will be *irregular*, and the more irregular the shapes are, the more interesting your mandala design is likely to be.

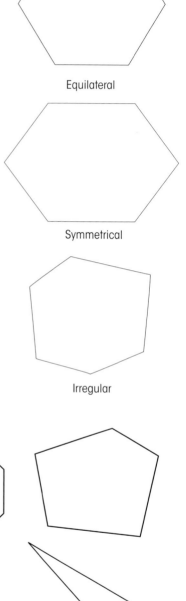

Equilateral

Symmetrical

Irregular

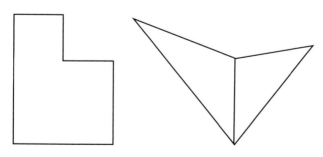

Shapes with curved sides like the two above will not work for spirals

A shape with inward-pointing corners like the one on the left will not work for a spiral. However, a shape with inward-pointing corners can be divided into multiple shapes with all corners pointing out, as in the shape on the right.

These shapes will work for spirals, because all corners point out.

58

PARTS OF SPIRALS

The basic parts of a spiral are triangles, rings, spokes and center.

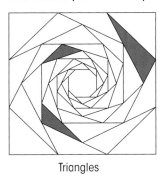 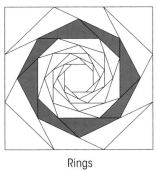 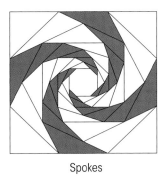 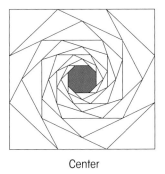

Triangles   Rings   Spokes   Center

Inside or inward means toward the center. Outside or outward means away from the center, toward the outer edge.

When you draw a spiral, you start at the outer edge of the shape and create rings of triangles going inward toward the center. When you sew a spiral, you start at the center and sew rings of triangles outward toward the outer edge.

A *clockwise* (C) spiral has spokes that curve clockwise from outer edge to center. A *counterclockwise* (X) spiral has spokes that curve counterclockwise from outer edge to center. (Refer to page 15 for a more detailed explanation of clockwise and counterclockwise.)

The *base* of a triangle is the side that sits toward the center. The peak of a triangle is the highest point across from the base. The height of a triangle is the distance from the base to the peak. The length of the shortest side of the triangle is the increment (Nesting and Pinwheel spirals only). The tip is the narrowest corner.

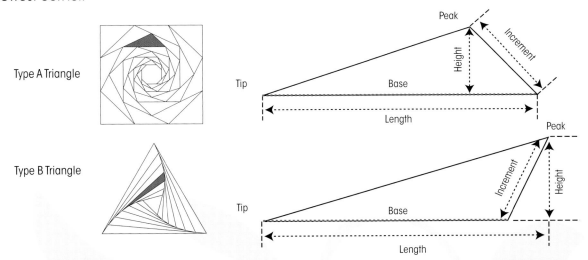

Type A Triangle

Type B Triangle

Type A Triangle: When the outer shape of a spiral has a corner angle of 90° (a right angle) or more, the base of the triangles in that spoke is the longest side, and the length of the triangles is the same as the base.

Type B Triangle: When the outer shape of a spiral has a corner angle of less than 90°, the peak of the triangles in that spoke extends beyond the base and the length of the triangles extends out as far out as the peak.

Knowing which side is the base of the triangle makes a difference when cutting the base on the grain of fabric and positioning fabric on the foundation (see pages 99–100).

TOOLS FOR DRAWING SPIRALS AND DRAFTING FOUNDATIONS

The tools for drawing spirals and drafting foundations mainly consist of regular office supplies and quilting tools you probably already have on hand.

- Thin 12" ruler that lays flat on the surface of the paper (this prevents a shadow, which makes it hard to see where you are placing the ruler)
- 24" rotary cutting ruler
- Mechanical pencil (my favorite is a Pentel P205)
- Black ultra-fine-point (not just fine, ultra-fine) permanent marker—I prefer Sharpie brand
- Red pen
- Eraser—the retractable stick type is best
- Correction-fluid pen
- Transparent tape—I prefer the ¾" Scotch brand in the green box because it doesn't melt when ironed at low to medium temperatures
- Double-sided tape—the permanent variety, not the removable
- Scissors for paper
- White drawing paper (use a sheet large enough to accommodate the whole wedge)
- Translucent foundation material—vellum or nonwoven sheets (see page 95 and Resources, page 157)

TECHNIQUES FOR ACCURATE DRAWING

When drawing a spiral, and particularly when drafting actual foundations, it's important that the lines are narrow (the width of a single thread is ideal) and the ends of the lines match up accurately. Accurate drawing leads to accurate sewing. Use these tools and simple techniques to set yourself up for success.

Always use the sharpest pencil or pen that you can. Pencil and pen widths vary, so use the same pencil or pen consistently throughout the drawing process to keep lines and measurements accurate. My favorite pencil is a Pentel P205. The metal shaft and thin lead allow the pencil to ride precisely along the edge of the ruler. The tip of this pencil is super-accurate, and the small built-in eraser is just the right size for erasing the lines in Pinwheel spirals.

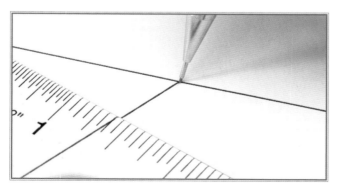

1 Use a mechanical pencil and thin, flat ruler. Place the tip of the pencil exactly where the line will start.

2 Push the ruler up against the pencil.

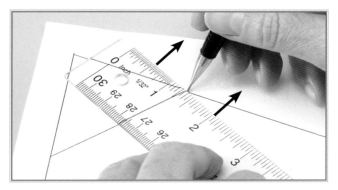

Wrong   Wrong   Right

3 Place the tip of the pencil where you want the line to end. Push the ruler up against the pencil there. Try not to move the ruler away from the starting point as you adjust it.

4 Place the pencil again on the starting point; adjust the ruler if needed. (Repeat as necessary at each end of the line until the ruler is positioned exactly at both points.) Draw the line. Let this technique become a habit and you will always have perfectly matching points.

NESTING SPIRALS

Nesting spirals fit in any shape, and they are the easiest spiral to draw and to sew. Because of these conveniences, most of the spirals you use in a mandala will be Nesting spirals.

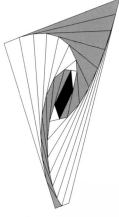

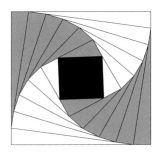

The traditional Twisted Log Cabin block shown above is a Nesting spiral in a square.

Like the Twisted Log Cabin block above, this spiral has four sides, but changing the proportions of the shape changes the proportions of the spokes. Long sides make petal-like spokes and short sides make thin, ribbon-like spokes.

Wind Power
Designed and pieced by Linda McGibbon, quilted by Carol Rose
8-wedge, rotational symmetry
17" × 23½"
This mandala is quite simple, with just one Nesting spiral in each wedge, which makes it easy to see the spiral.

HOW TO DRAW A NESTING SPIRAL
Drawing a nesting spiral is as easy as connecting dot-to-dot.

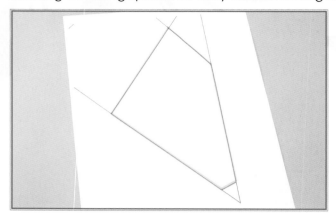

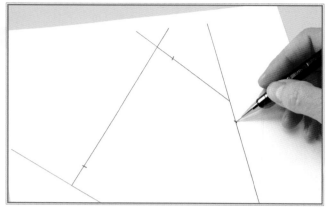

1 Select the shape within the wedge where you are going to draw a spiral. Remember that all corners of the shape must point out. (The area I will be working in for this demonstration has been highlighted in yellow.) Decide if you want the spiral to spin clockwise (C) or counterclockwise (X). Once you choose a direction, work in the same direction for the entire spiral.

2 Begin the spiral by marking the first increments. Moving from each corner in the direction you chose, mark a dot on each side of the shape between the corner and the center of each side. The distance between the corner and the dot is the *increment*.

As you work, don't pass the center of the side, as this can cause the spiral to change direction. If you are drawing a full-sized mandala, the increment will usually be between ¾"–1½". If you are drawing a wedge puzzle in a 10" wedge, the increment will be about ½"–¾". You may measure the increment if you wish, but you don't have to. The increments can be different lengths on different sides of the shape. (You can alter the proportions of a spiral by adjusting the placement of increment dots. See pages 65 and 79–82 for more on this.)

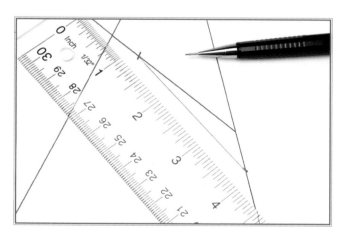

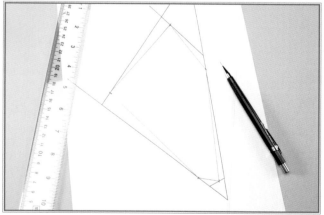

3 Use the ruler to connect dot to dot in order around the shape until a ring of triangles is formed. Make sure the ends of the lines meet accurately at the dots on the sides of the shape. Inside the ring of triangles should be a new

shape with the same number of sides as the original shape. (If your new shape doesn't have the same number of sides as the previous one, you either skipped a side or you mixed up the direction of the dots.)

Important Note

When drafting Nesting or Baravelle spirals in a full-size wedge foundation, draw the first ring of all spirals in the wedge before completing individual spirals. Align connecting increment dots in fan flow forms, both within the spiral and along the edges of the wedge, then complete each spiral. (See Connecting Spirals, page 89 for more detail.)

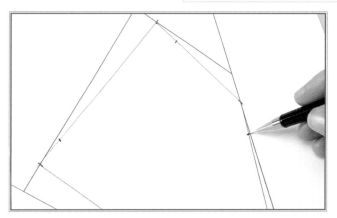

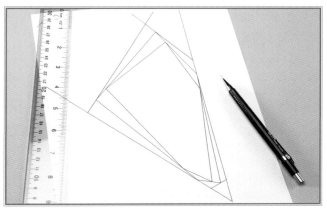

4 Repeat Step 2 to mark increments on the new shape that formed inside the previous one. Mark the dots in the same direction from the corners of the new shape as the first set of dots. For a smooth, balanced spiral, use the same increment as you did in Step 2. For a more freeform spiral, you can vary the increment lengths, but don't pass the middle of the side of the shape.

5 Repeat Step 3, connecting the new set of dots to form a second ring of triangles. You may find it helpful to draw this second ring of triangles in a different color.

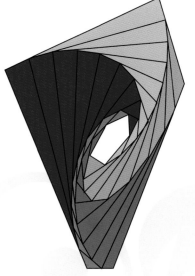

6 After several repetitions of Steps 2–3, you will see the spokes of the spiral being formed by the adjacent triangles in successive rings. Continue making new rings until the center of the spiral is the size you desire.

7 Place the same color in the triangles that share long sides to color the spokes. Another way to look at it is that the edges of the spokes follow the short sides of the triangles.

When you're sketching and designing:

Nesting spirals work best in shapes with 3–6 sides.

For a wedge puzzle, use Nesting spirals to represent both Nesting spirals and Pinwheel spirals. Nesting spirals are much easier to draw, so they can serve as placeholders for Pinwheel spirals in the wedge puzzle until the drafting stage, when you'll choose whether to use Nesting or Pinwheel spirals. In the first ring of triangles in each shape, use the same increment on all sides of the shape so that fan flow forms will connect smoothly.

When you're drafting:

When you begin drafting the actual foundations, decide whether a Nesting or Pinwheel spiral is the best choice for the design. The advantages and disadvantages of each type are listed on pages 66–67. You can also create a hybrid spiral that combines the advantages of both (see page 82).

Use a Nesting spiral at the point of a wedge to avoid excess bulk at the center of the mandala where multiple seams meet. (A hybrid spiral may also be a good choice here.)

Nesting spirals are split-side spirals—the triangles do not completely cover the sides of the outer shape. Because of this, they may require special attention when they connect to other spirals. (See Connecting Spirals, page 89 for more details.)

When you're sewing:

Nesting spirals are the easiest spirals to sew (see pages 104–105). They can be sewn several triangles at a time, as long as the triangles don't touch. (Baravelle spirals are sewn the same way.)

Quilts in this book that use Nesting spirals:

With the exception of *A New Spin on the Snail's Trail* (page 36), every quilt in this book uses at least some (if not all) Nesting spirals. Some good examples are:

The Zebras Went Crazy, page 150
A Summer on Grant Island, page 152
Flow Blue, page 154

Flutter by the Garden

Designed, pieced and quilted by Susan Arnold
12-wedge, mirror symmetry
48" × 52"

Nesting spirals may be the simplest type of spiral, but Susan's quilt—made only with Nesting spirals—proves that they can produce sophisticated designs. In this mandala, strategic placement of gradations and split flow forms create the illusion of two stars layered over one another. Do you see the orange butterflies that give the quilt its theme? (Hint: look between 1:00 and 3:00.)

Choosing an Increment for Nesting and Pinwheel Spirals

How Long Should the Increment Be?

When drawing a Nesting or Pinwheel spiral, you can place increment dots anywhere between the corner and the center of the side of the shape. Think of this as the "increment zone." Don't pass the center of the side as this can sometimes cause the spiral to change direction.

   The height of the triangle (red arrows below) is often more important than the length of the increment (blue arrows below), because keeping a fairly consistent triangle height throughout a mandala creates a proportionate and unified design. Place increments closer to the corner of the shape for a lower triangle (diagram on left), and further from the corner for a higher triangle (diagram on right).

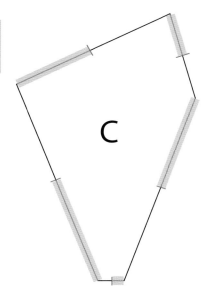

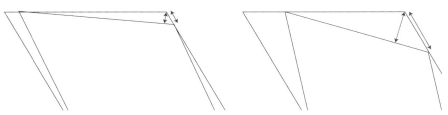

The diagram above shows the increment zone for this clockwise spiral. The increment zone for a counterclockwise spiral would be the unmarked portion of each side.

Triangle height is also affected by angles at the corners of the shape. When the corner of a shape has a very wide angle, short increments at that corner will create very low triangles (top right diagram). For higher triangles, use longer increments (bottom right diagram).

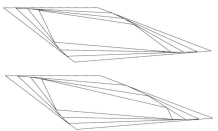

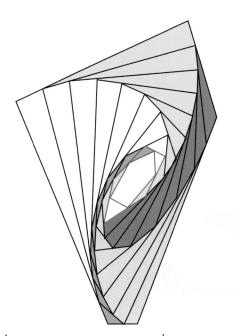

Here are some situations where you might want to adjust increment length:

For a smooth, evenly flowing spiral, you can (1) maintain a consistent increment within each spoke as shown in the white spoke at left, or (2) maintain consistent triangle height in a spoke by adjusting the increment as necessary as shown in the blue spoke at left.

   The sides of the shapes become shorter near the center of the spiral, and eventually become too short to accommodate the increment length you started with. When this happens, simply place the increment dot at the center of the side as in a Baravelle spiral (this is indicated with red lines at the center of the diagram at left). Continue drawing rings until the center reaches the size you desire.

   Triangles near the center of the spiral become smaller as well. Adjust increments and height as necessary to keep these triangles proportionate to the spoke and the overall design (see the yellow spoke at left for an example).

   When the side of a shape is very short, it creates a thin ribbony spoke like the green one at left. You can't widen these spokes much, but lengthening the increment to raise the height of the triangles helps. If you want to avoid these, lengthen the side of the shape where the spoke begins.

   Adjusting an increment to create a large triangle is a way to make room for a fussy-cut motif.

Other creative increment adjustments:

Steer the curve of one or more spokes in a Pinwheel spiral (see page 79).
Draw an off-center spiral: Pinwheel or Nesting (see page 80).

NESTING VERSUS PINWHEEL SPIRALS

What's the difference between Nesting and Pinwheel spirals? In Nesting spirals, the tips of the triangles don't extend all the way to the corner of the shape. In Pinwheel spirals, the tips of the triangles do extend into the corner of the shape. This factor affects your design in three ways: bulk, design and sewing. I recommend using a Nesting spiral whenever possible; however, if the design advantages of a Pinwheel spiral improve your design, use a Pinwheel spiral. If you need the design advantages of a Pinwheel spiral as well as the bulk and sewing advantages of a Nesting spiral, try a hybrid spiral (see page 82).

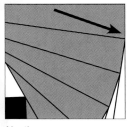 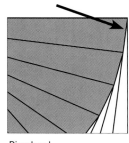

Nesting   Pinwheel

	NESTING	PINWHEEL
Bulk (Best choice: Nesting)	Nesting spirals are the better choice for minimizing bulk. Since they do not have seams in the corners, less bulk builds up where corners meet. Use Nesting spirals in the center of a mandala, in fan flow forms and at any other place where you have the corners of several shapes coming together.	Since the seams of Pinwheel spirals extend into the corners of the shape, they place several layers of fabric in a narrow point. The layers of fabric especially build up when the points of several triangles fall close together. If you place bulky points of two Pinwheel spirals side-by-side in a fan or point flow form, the bulk problem compounds even more. If you try to put multiple bulky points together at the center of a mandala, you'll have a big problem.
Design (Best choice: depends on design)	**Connections:** Nesting spirals have split sides—each side of the outer shape is covered by two triangles. Sometimes this complicates connections between spirals (see page 89). **Trunk Flow Forms:** Trunk flow forms (see page 20) between Nesting spirals sometimes end up looking narrow and spindly. If a trunk flow form isn't solid enough for your design, change one or both spirals to Pinwheel spirals, or use a hybrid spiral with a Pinwheel side against the trunk flow form (see page 82). **Steering curves:** Nesting spirals cannot be steered, so they do not allow you to control the curve of spokes and flow forms (see page 79).	**Connections:** Pinwheel spirals have solid sides—each side of the outer shape is covered by a single triangle. This sometimes makes for nicer connections between spirals (see page 89). **Trunk Flow Forms:** A trunk flow form (see page 20) between Pinwheel spirals is a more solid shape. Bulk is not a problem here, because the bulky points of each Pinwheel spiral sit against a side, not a point, of the other spiral. **Steering curves:** Pinwheel spirals allow you to control the curve of spokes and flow forms (see page 79).
Sewing (Best choice: Nesting)	Nesting spirals are quicker and easier to sew than Pinwheel spirals (see pages 104–105). With Nesting spirals, you can sew all the even-numbered triangles in one step, then all the odd-numbered triangles in one step (or in two, if the shape has an uneven number of sides).	With Pinwheel spirals, you must sew one triangle at a time in order around the spiral, then finish with a partial seam, which takes more time and concentration (see pages 106–108).

PINWHEEL SPIRALS

Pinwheel spirals fit in any shape and are very similar to Nesting spirals. The main difference is that the triangles in Pinwheel spirals completely cover the side of the shape, while the triangles in Nesting spirals only cover part of the shape.

When drafting your design, always try Nesting spirals first, because they are easier to draw and sew. But if a Pinwheel spiral improves the design—by making a stronger connection between spirals, or steering the curve of a spoke, for example—use a Pinwheel spiral instead.

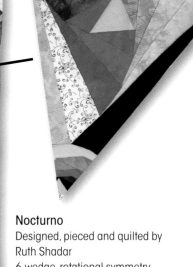

Nocturno
Designed, pieced and quilted by
Ruth Shadar
6-wedge, rotational symmetry
40" × 40"
This mandala is striking despite its simple structure—a single Pinwheel spiral makes up each wedge. A Baravelle spiral forms the center, and a group of spirals forms one corner of the border. The off-center placement of the mandala on the background and the "broken" upper right-hand corner give the impression that this mandala has just crashed into the frame as it hurtles through space.

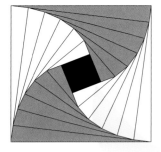

A Pinwheel spiral in a square is another version of the traditional Twisted Log Cabin block.

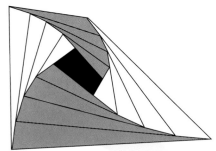

A Pinwheel spiral will fit in any shape. Like the Twisted Log Cabin block at left, this spiral has four sides, but changing the proportions of the shape changes the proportions of the spokes. A long side, like the bottom of this shape, makes a petal-like spoke; a short side, such as the top of this shape, makes a thinner spoke.

HOW TO DRAW A PINWHEEL SPIRAL

The process of drawing a Pinwheel spiral starts out the same as drawing a Nesting spiral, but changes when you get to connecting the increment dots.

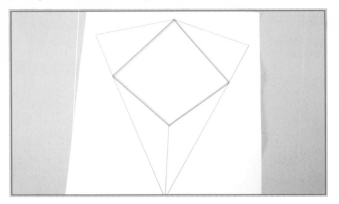

1 Select the shape within the wedge where you are going to draw a spiral. Remember that all corners of the shape must point out. (The area I will be working in for this demonstration has been highlighted in yellow.) Decide if you want the spiral to spin clockwise (C) or counterclockwise (X). Once you choose a direction, work in the same direction for the entire spiral.

2 Begin the spiral by marking the first set of increments. Move from each corner in the direction you chose, and mark a dot on each side of the shape between the corner and the center of each side (don't pass the center of the side, as this can cause the spiral to change direction). If you are drawing a full-sized mandala, the increment will usually be between ¾"–1½". If you are drawing in a 10" wedge, the increment will be about ½"–¾". You can measure the increment if you wish, but you don't have to. The increments can be different lengths on different sides of the shape. (You can alter the proportions of a spiral by adjusting the placement of increment dots. See pages 65 and 79–82 for more on this.)

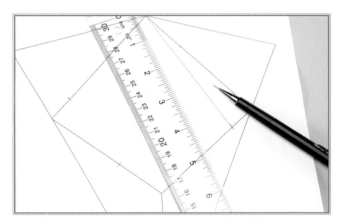

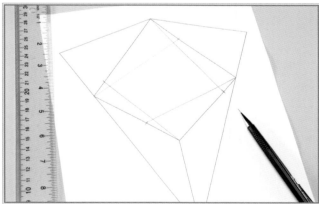

3 To connect each dot to a corner of the shape first, put one index finger on a dot. Then, with the other index finger, start at the dot, and trace around the edge of the shape in the opposite direction you chose in Step 1. Stop at the second corner you come to. Use the ruler to draw a line between this corner and the dot where you started to create a triangle. Make sure

the ends of the lines meet the corners and the dots precisely.

Repeat this process for each dot, working in order around the shape. (It helps to turn the paper as you work.) As you go around the shape, the new lines will cross the tips of the triangles you drew before them.

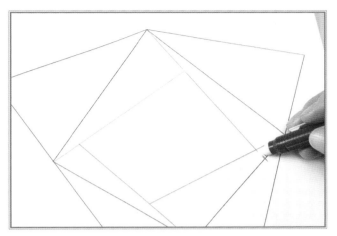

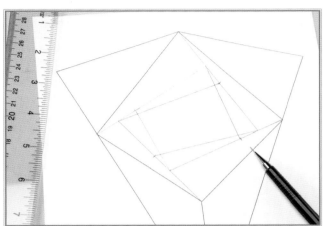

4 To complete the first ring of triangles, erase the short bits of line that cross the tip of each triangle. (When you get more comfortable drawing Pinwheel spirals, you can end each line where it meets the previous line, so you won't have to go back and erase the crossovers.)

When you're done, you'll see a ring of triangles with the short side of each triangle laying against a long side of the triangle next to it. There is a new shape inside the ring with the same number of sides as the original shape.

5 Working inside the new shape, repeat Steps 2–4, marking dots, connecting dots to corners and erasing unneeded lines to form a second ring of triangles. Mark the increments in the same direction as for the first ring. You may find it helpful to use a different color to draw each new ring of triangles.

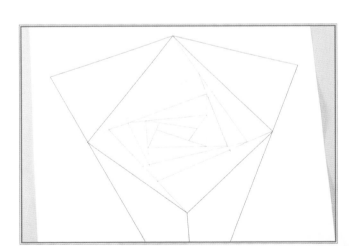

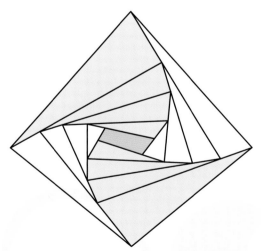

6 Repeat Steps 2–5 for additional rings, each time working inside the new ring you just drew. After several repetitions you will see the spokes of the spiral being formed by the adjacent triangles in successive rings.

7 To finish, color the spiral. Place the same color in the triangles that share long sides to color the spokes. Another way to look at it is that the edges of the spokes follow the short sides of the triangles.

HELPFUL HINTS ABOUT PINWHEEL SPIRALS

When you're sketching and designing:
Don't use Pinwheel spirals in a wedge puzzle—Nesting spirals are much faster and easier for this purpose. (You'll choose between Nesting and Pinwheel spirals later, when you draft the wedge full size.)

When you're drafting:
Pinwheel spirals work best in shapes with 3–6 sides.

Pinwheel spirals are full-side spirals—the triangles completely cover the sides of the outer shape. They usually connect to other spirals without any special adjustments (see page 89).

In Pinwheel spirals, like Nesting spirals, you can control the height of the triangles by adjusting the placement of the increment dot. In Pinwheel spirals, this allows you to steer the curves of the spokes (see page 79).

Use Pinwheel spirals only when you need them for their design advantages. Otherwise, they add unnecessary bulk to seams.

When you're sewing:
Pinwheel spirals must be sewn one triangle at a time in order around the ring. The first triangle has a partial seam that is finished after the last triangle—the same sewing technique as Point-to-Point spirals (see pages 106–108).

Quilts in this book that use Pinwheel spirals:
October Glory, page 30
Fireball, page 40
Supernova, page 40
Cosmic Spin, page 43
Magnetic Moments, page 46
Easter Mandala, page 124 (Lily spiral)

Reflections
Designed, pieced and quilted by
Holly Watson
12-wedge, compound mirror symmetry
24" × 29"
Holly made this small oval mandala to practice before she began *The Zebras Went Crazy* (page 150). She used all Pinwheel spirals and learned that it would have been much easier to make using Nesting spirals, both because of the more complicated process of sewing Pinwheel spirals, and because of the bulk where spirals joined.

BARAVELLE SPIRALS

The "twirliest" of all the spirals, Baravelle spirals can spin equally either clockwise or counterclockwise and even in both directions at the same time. They are sewn in the same manner as Nesting spirals.

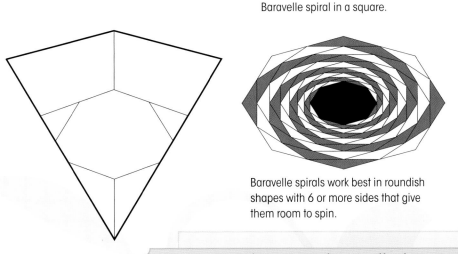

The traditional Snail's Trail block is a Baravelle spiral in a square.

Baravelle spirals work best in roundish shapes with 6 or more sides that give them room to spin.

Blueberry Swirl Sundae

Designed, pieced and quilted by Susan Ott
6-wedge, mirror and rotational symmetry
24½" diameter

Susan liked this mandala so well she made *I Think I'm Losing My Marbles* (page 155) from the same design. The wedge is a Type 2 symmetrical wedge (see page 35) that is divided symmetrically down the middle except for a large, full-width octagon that is perfect for holding a large Baravelle (or Point-to-Point) spiral. Mirrored pairs of spirals in the divided sections of the wedge combined with single-direction Baravelle spirals give this design its combination of mirror and rotational symmetry. Compare this mandala and wedge to *Sultana* (page 144), *Dancing Calla Lilies* (page 75) and *Cosmic Spin* (page 43).

Why are They Called Baravelle Spirals?

Baravelle spirals are named for James Baravelle (pronounced BEAR a vell), the eighteenth-century mathematician who discovered them.

71

HOW TO DRAW A BARAVELLE SPIRAL

Drawing a Baravelle spiral is almost the same as drawing a Nesting spiral. The difference is that in a Nesting spiral you place the increment dots before the middle of the side of the shape, while in a Baravelle spiral you place the increment dots exactly at the middle. This is why Baravelle spirals can spin in both directions.

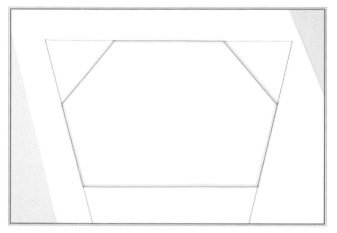

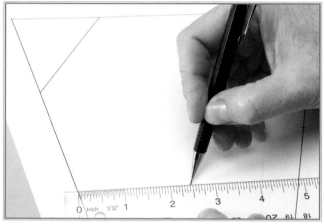

1 Select the shape within the wedge where you are going to draw this spiral. Make sure all corners of the shape are pointing out. (Above, I've highlighted the shape I'll be working in.)

For a Baravelle spiral, you do not need to decide which direction it will spin, because it spins equally in both directions. You'll determine the direction when you color it.

2 On each side of the shape, mark a dot at the exact center of the side so it is divided in half. You can measure this with a ruler or fold the line in half to mark the center point of the side.

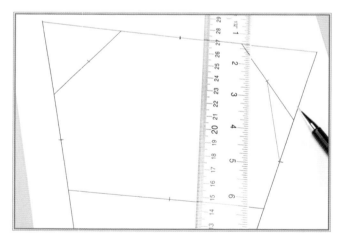

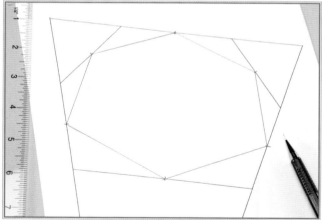

3 Use the ruler to connect dot to dot in order around the shape to form a ring of triangles that touch at the tips. Make sure the ends of the lines meet accurately at the dots on the side of the shape. You now see a new shape inside the

first one with the same number of sides as the original shape. (If your new shape doesn't have the same number of sides as the previous one, you skipped a side.)

When drafting Nesting or Baravelle spirals in a full-size wedge foundation, draw the first ring of all spirals in the wedge before completing individual spirals. Align connecting increment dots in fan flow forms, both within the spiral and along the edges of the wedge, then complete each spiral. (See Connecting Spirals, page 89 for more detail.)

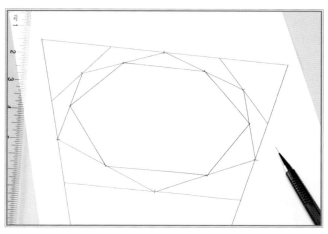

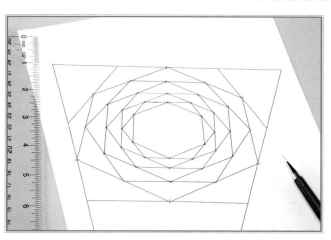

4 Repeat Steps 2–3, this time marking the midpoints of the sides of the new shape inside the previous one. This forms a new ring of triangles inside the first one.

5 Repeat Steps 2–3 several times to finish the spiral. (If you don't see a spiral yet, don't worry, you will in the next step).

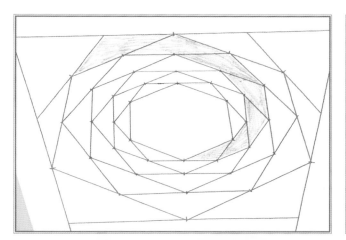

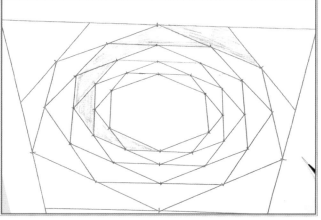

Clockwise

Counterclockwise

6 A Baravelle spiral can spin either clockwise or counterclockwise—just color the spokes in the direction you want. Start from a triangle on the outside edge, and notice that two triangles in the next ring each cover half of its base (the long side). Of these two triangles, select the triangle that moves in the direction you want the spiral to spin and color it in. Continue in the same direction all the way to the center of the spiral. Another way to look at it is that the edges of the spokes follow the short sides of the triangles in either direction you choose.

HELPFUL HINTS ABOUT BARAVELLE SPIRALS

When you're sketching and designing:

Use Baravelle spirals in your mandala where you want a very twirly spiral. With Baravelles, you'll see spokes more than flow forms.

Baravelle spirals should not be used in long, narrow shapes or shapes with sharp pointed corners. However, you can cut off a corner to round out a shape in order to accommodate a Baravelle spiral.

Baravelle spirals spin equally in both directions, so you only need to draw one Baravelle spiral in a shape of a wedge puzzle to make both clockwise and counterclockwise spirals. After drawing one spiral, make a copy. In one copy, lightly shade in a spoke or two spinning clockwise and in the other shade a spoke or two spinning counterclockwise.

When drawing a wedge puzzle, use Baravelle spirals only when you want the specific look or proportions of a Baravelle spiral.

When you're drafting:

Baravelle spirals are split-side spirals—the triangles do not completely cover the sides of the outside shape. So, they require special attention when connecting them to other spirals (see pages 89–91).

In Baravelle spirals, the proportions of the triangles and the overall spiral are set by drawing to the midpoint of each side. You cannot vary the triangles within the spiral or the proportions of the spiral.

Baravelle spirals and Nesting spirals are "first cousins." They can easily be combined to help make a smooth connection between Baravelles and other spirals.

When you're sewing:

Baravelle spirals are sewn like Nesting spirals—you can sew several triangles at a time, as long as the triangles don't touch (see pages 104–105).

Quilts in this book that use Baravelle spirals:

A New Spin on the Snail's Trail, page 36
Supernova, page 40 (center)
Magnetic Moments, page 46
Nocturno, page 67 (center)
Blueberry Swirl Sundae, page 71
Sultana, page 144
Renaissance Dreams, page 152
I Think I'm Losing My Marbles, page 155

Gemini Rose

Designed, pieced and quilted by
Kerry Hansing
3-wedge, rotational symmetry
35" diameter
This mandala is completely different from any other in the book because the three rose spirals sit completely independent of each other without connecting to any other part of the design. These Baravelle spirals spin clockwise except for a single black spoke that spins counterclockwise.

POINT-TO-POINT SPIRALS

Point-to-Point spirals are drawn by connecting the corners of the shape, so they work only in shapes with five or more sides. They have more spin than Nesting or Pinwheel spirals, but less than Baravelles. Linked flow forms in Point-to-Point spirals can form beautiful flowing ribbons.

Dancing Calla Lilies
Designed and pieced by Linda McGibbon, quilted by Carol Rose
12-wedge, compound mirror symmetry, changing spiral direction
55" × 55"
Linked Point-to-Point spirals create the exquisite black and brick-red ribbons that circle Linda's mandala. For me, this is one of the most intriguing and inspiring designs in this book. Study the symmetry: As you move outward from the center, you first find simple mirror symmetry pairs. Then, there's a compound mirror symmetry group of two wedges that divides the overall symmetry in thirds. Finally, a different compound mirror symmetry group of three wedges divides the symmetry into quarters. Ultimately, the only way that the complete mandala can be divided into perfectly symmetrical sections is vertically down the middle.

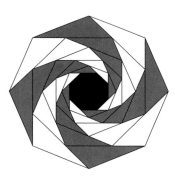

Point-to-Point spirals work best in roundish shapes with 6 or more sides; this gives them room to spin.

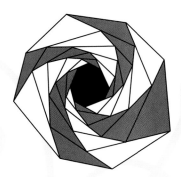

Even in an irregular shape, the Point-to-Point spiral still works.

HOW TO DRAW A POINT-TO-POINT SPIRAL

There are two methods for drawing Point-to-Point Spirals.
Try Method A and Method B to see which works better for you.

Drawing a Point-to-Point Spiral—Method A

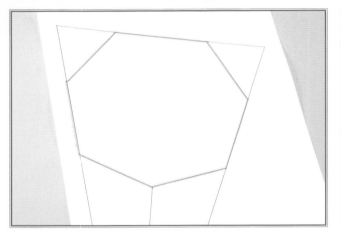

1 Select the shape within the wedge where you are going to draw this spiral. Remember, all corners of the shape must point out. (Here, I've highlighted the shape I'll be working in.)

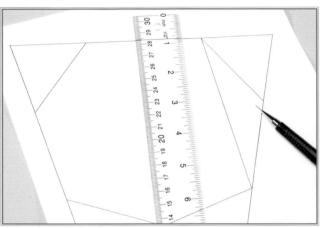

2 Choose any corner of the shape and call it the first corner. Working in either direction, draw a line connecting the first corner to the third corner. Make sure the end of the line meets the corner precisely.

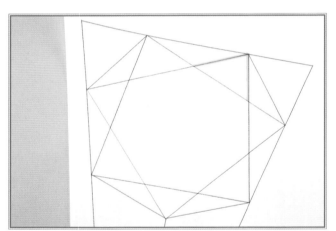

3 Working in either direction, continue to draw lines to connect every other corner until you arrive back where you started. If the shape has an uneven number of sides, one trip around the shape will connect all the corners. If the shape has an even number of sides, one trip around the shape will connect half the corners, so start at an empty corner and repeat this step to connect the rest.

Every corner of the outer shape now has two lines that extend inward from the corner and cross a line (one example of these lines has been highlighted above for clarity). You're going to erase one of these two lines at each corner.

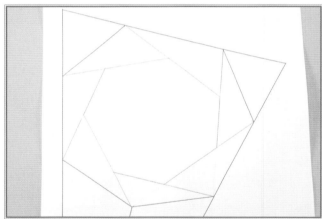

4 Choose either the lines on the counterclockwise side to create a clockwise-spinning spiral, as shown here, or choose the lines on the clockwise side to create a counterclockwise-spinning spiral. (Mark the lines you chose to erase with a pencil to help avoid confusion when you start erasing.) At each corner, erase the line you marked, from the corner to where it crosses another line. As you erase, a ring of triangles appears with the short side of each triangle adjoining the long side of the triangle next to it. Follow Steps 5–6 on page 78 to complete the Point-to-Point spiral.

Drawing a Point-to-Point Spiral—Method B

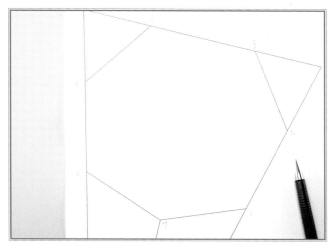

1 Select the shape within the wedge where you are going to draw this spiral (see Step 1 of Method A on the previous page). Number the corners of the shape in order around the outer edge. Number clockwise for a counterclockwise-spinning spiral and counterclockwise for a clockwise-spinning spiral.

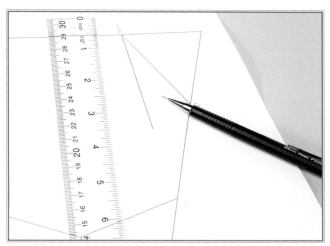

2 Align your ruler with corners 1 and 3. Starting at corner 3, draw a line toward corner 1, stopping about ¾ of the distance to corner 1.

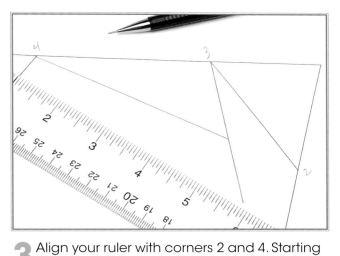

3 Align your ruler with corners 2 and 4. Starting at corner 4, draw a line toward corner 2, stopping where it meets the line you just drew between corners 1 and 3.

4 Repeat Step 3 for corners 3 and 5, corners 4 and 6, etc., drawing the line from the higher numbered corner toward the lower numbered corner, until you arrive back at the first triangle. (The next-to-last line will go from corner 1 toward the next to last number, and the last line will go from corner 2 toward the last number.) Close up the space between the end of the first line and the last line (or erase the first line it overlaps the last). As you draw lines, a ring of triangles appears, with the short side of each triangle adjoining the long side of the triangle next to it. Follow Steps 5–6 on page 78 to complete the Point-to-Point spiral.

Finishing a Point-to-Point Spiral—Methods A and B

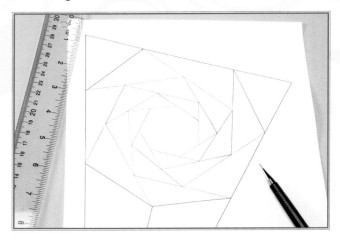

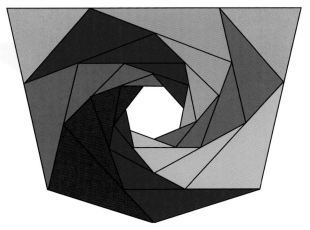

5 Repeat Steps 2–4 several times, each time in the new shape that forms inside the previous one. If using Method A, erase the line in the same direction each time. (You may find it helpful to use a different color to draw each new ring of triangles.) After several repetitions you will see the spokes of the spiral formed by the adjacent triangles in successive rings.

6 To color the spiral, find the edges of the spokes by following the short sides of the triangles, then fill in the spokes.

HELPFUL HINTS ABOUT POINT-TO-POINT SPIRALS

When you're sketching and designing:
Point-to-Point spirals are best used in roundish shapes with 6 or more sides that give them room to spin. They should not be used in long, narrow shapes or shapes with sharp pointed corners. However, you can cut off a corner in order to round out a shape to accommodate a Point-to-Point spiral.

Linking Point-to-Point spirals around a mandala can create the effect of twisting ribbons.

In a wedge puzzle, use Point-to-Point spirals only when you want the specific look or proportions of a Point-to-Point spiral.

When you're drafting:
Point-to-Point spirals are full-side spirals—the triangles completely cover the sides of the outside shape. They usually connect to other spirals without any special adjustments (see pages 89–91).

The proportions of a Point-to-Point Spiral are set by using the corners of the shape to draw them, so you cannot vary the triangles within the spiral the way you can in a Nesting or Pinwheel Spiral.

When you're sewing:
Point-to-Point spirals require a sewing technique different from Nesting and Baravelle spirals (see pages 106–108). They must be sewn one triangle at a time in order around the ring. The first triangle has a partial seam that is finished after the last triangle. (Point-to-Point and Pinwheel spirals are sewn in the same way.)

Another quilt in this book that uses Point-to-Point spirals:
Fireball, page 40 (center)

ADVANCED SPIRAL TECHNIQUES

Once you are comfortable drawing spirals, there are many options for adjusting their proportions—steering a Pinwheel spiral, drafting a hybrid spiral and drafting an off-center spiral are all outlined here. Use these options when you want to take more control of the shape of a flow form in your design.

Another useful technique to learn at this point is how to reduce the center seams of your spiral. Reducing bulk now will make assembling your mandala much easier later on.

STEERING A PINWHEEL SPIRAL

When drawing the Lily spiral in *Easter Mandala* (page 124), I found that a Nesting spiral didn't give me the shape I wanted. So instead, I used a Pinwheel spiral and "steered" the curves of the spokes that form the lily.

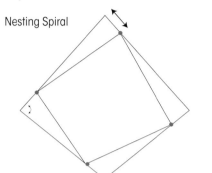

Nesting Spiral

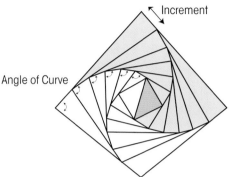

Increment

Angle of Curve

The diagrams above show a Nesting spiral. When you draw a Nesting spiral, you place the increment dots (marked here by a straight arrow), then draw a line connecting each dot to the next dot. This creates a ring of triangles where the shortest side of each triangle is part of the side of the shape in which it is drawn. This is important because whatever the angle is at the corner of the shape (marked above by a curved arrow), that is the angle at which the spoke curves—the *angle of curve* for that spoke—at that point. You can't change this angle of curve because it is determined and locked in by the corner of the previous shape. You can change the increments, but you can't change the angle of curve. This happens on every corner, every spoke and every shape (whether the shape is the outer shape or any of the interior ones) as you draw toward the center of the spiral.

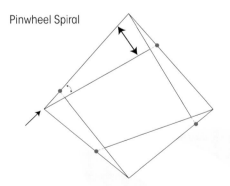

Pinwheel Spiral

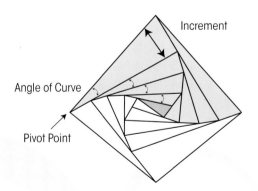

Increment

Angle of Curve

Pivot Point

Note: The centers of these spirals are split from corner to corner to make the continuous white line and the yellow center of the flower.

Now look at the Pinwheel spiral. When you draw a Pinwheel spiral, you place the increment dots (marked by a straight double-headed arrow) and then you draw lines from the corners of the shape to the dots, stopping where the line bumps into the neighboring line. This means that each line can pivot at its corner (marked by a single-headed arrow). So, you can adjust the angle of curve (marked by a curved arrow) by anchoring the line at the corner of the shape and changing the increment. This is how you "steer" the curve of the spoke throughout the spiral. By steering the curves of the spokes in the Pinwheel spiral, I was able to create a spiral that looks like a lily.

DRAFTING AN OFF-CENTER NESTING OR PINWHEEL SPIRAL

You can move the center of a Nesting or Pinwheel spiral off-center to change the curves and proportions of all the spokes in the spiral and the flow forms that connect to it. The example here uses a Nesting spiral.

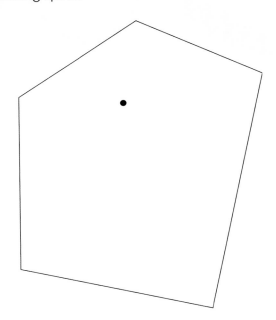

1 Mark a dot inside the shape where you want the center of the spiral to sit. (Remember, the center is a smaller shape that will sit around this dot. The spokes will not meet on this dot.)

2 Measure the distance from the center dot to the nearest corner of the shape, and write this measurement by that corner. Label this corner X.

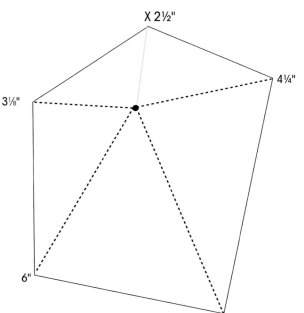

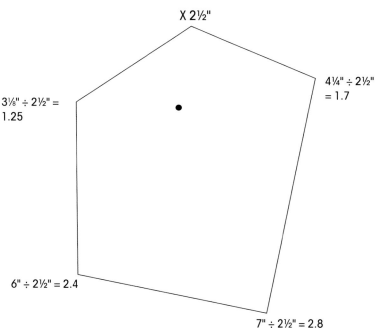

3 Measure the distance from the center dot to every other corner, and write each measurement by its corresponding corner.

4 Take the measurement from corner X and divide every other center-to-corner measurement by that number. Write the outcome by its corresponding corner. This is the increment ratio. (You can now erase the first measurement you wrote by each corner.)

80

X Increment = ½"

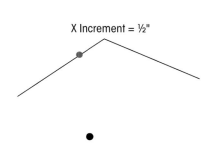

X Increment = ½"

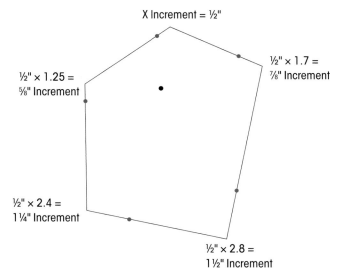

½" × 1.25 =
⅝" Increment

½" × 1.7 =
⅞" Increment

½" × 2.4 =
1¼" Increment

½" × 2.8 =
1½" Increment

5 Decide which direction you want the spiral to spin. Begin drawing the spiral by marking the first increment dot for corner X. It can be any length you wish—here I am using a ½" increment. Measure and make a note of the length of the corner X increment.

6 To place the other increment dots, take the length of the corner X increment and multiply it by the increment ratio at each corner. Round the answer up to the nearest ⅛" using the fraction to decimal conversion chart below. This gives you the increment length for that corner. Write each increment length by its corresponding corner and mark the increment for each corner.

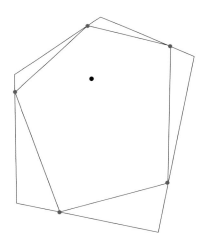

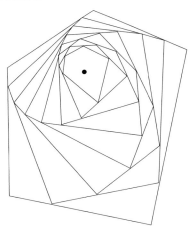

7 Connect the dots for the first ring of triangles.

8 Draw more rings, using the same increment at its corresponding corner for every ring of triangles. When a side of the spiral becomes too short to use the increment, simply place the increment dot at the center of the side of the shape, as you would for a Baravelle spiral. Don't place the increment dot past the center of the side of the shape, because this can change the direction of the spiral.

After doing this a few times, you'll develop a sense for the increment lengths needed to shift the center to where you want it, and you can estimate the increments without having to do the math.

Fraction to Decimal Conversion Chart

⅛" = .125	⅝" = .625
¼" = .25	¾" = .75
⅜" = .375	⅞" = .875
½" = .5	

DRAWING HYBRID SPIRALS

Nesting and Pinwheel spirals are quite similar in structure and proportion. This means that you can combine some Nesting-style spokes and some Pinwheel-style spokes in the same spiral to blend the best features of both types. This creates a hybrid spiral.

The example shown here is the point spiral from *Sultana* (page 144). It combines a Nesting spoke on one side of the spiral—to reduce bulk at the point—with Pinwheel spokes on the other sides—to steer a spoke. This type of hybrid is great for spirals at the center of a mandala. It can also eliminate the need for the partial-seam piecing that usually has to be done in a Pinwheel spiral. To sew this hybrid spiral, begin sewing each ring at the Nesting spoke. Sew in order around the ring as for a Pinwheel spiral, but there will be no partial seam to finish at the end of the ring.

Different types of spirals can be also be used in different rings (as opposed to different spokes) of the same spiral, as well. For more about this, read Connecting Spirals on pages 89–91.

1 Begin by marking increment dots exactly as you would for a Nesting or Pinwheel spiral.

2 On whichever side you want the Nesting spoke, connect the first two dots, dot to dot, as you would for a Nesting spiral.

3 Connect the remaining dots (shown here in blue) corner to dot as you would for a Pinwheel spiral.

4 Erase the lines that cut off the tips of the triangles as for a Pinwheel spiral. Also mark where the Nesting spoke begins.

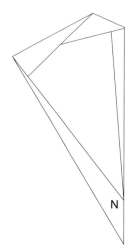

5 If you wish, adjust any of the lines drawn as Pinwheel spirals to steer that curve.

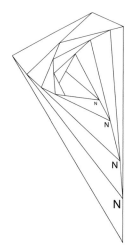

6 Complete the spiral, drawing each ring in the same way.

REDUCING CENTER SEAMS

All of the wedges come together at the center of the mandala. The more wedges, the more seams—and bulk—you'll have to manage. Besides using Nesting and hybrid spirals instead of Pinwheel spirals to keep seam allowances from piling up, use the techniques here to eliminate even more seams. You can also use these techniques other places in the mandala where you'd like to reduce bulk.

Cut-Off Point

In two adjoining spirals, cross the tips of both spirals with a single piece of fabric. Sew both complete spirals and join them (yellow line in illustrations at right), then sew the shared piece across the bottom (red dashed line) for a shared tip. You can even decide to add this shared tip after spirals are sewn and joined. Simply sew a piece of fabric across the tips of the joined spirals, trim it to the shape of the tip, then cut away the old tips behind the new shared tip.

Wrap-Over Point

In two adjoining spirals that make either a fan or a trunk flow form, draft the last ring of one spiral with a piece that wraps over the other spiral. Sew both complete spirals, but leave the end of the wrap-over piece partially unsewn (along the red dashed line in the illustrations at right). Join the pair of spirals (along the yellow line), then sew the wrap-over piece across the bottom of the other spiral. Trim to shape.

Double-Wide Point

In an upside-down fan flow form, draft the adjoining triangles as a single diamond-shaped piece. Sew this double-wide piece to one of the spirals. When joining the spirals, sew a shallow Y seam at the top of the diamond (yellow line in the illustrations at right). This method is particularly useful for fussy cutting fabrics with symmetrical designs, because there is no center seam to match. It's great for creating a kaleidoscopic star at the center of a mandala (see *Crest of the Crane*, page 120).

Appliqué Center

A fourth method is to eliminate the tips of the wedges at the center of the mandala altogether and simply appliqué a piece of fabric over the opening at the center of the mandala (see *Elizabeth*, page 128).

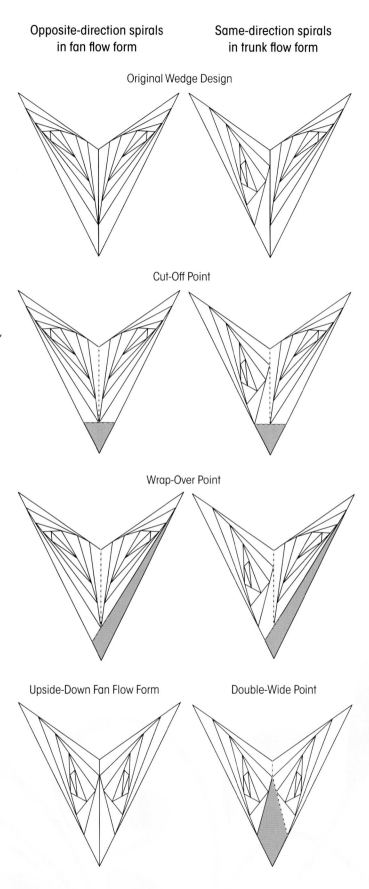

Opposite-direction spirals in fan flow form   Same-direction spirals in trunk flow form

Original Wedge Design

Cut-Off Point

Wrap-Over Point

Upside-Down Fan Flow Form   Double-Wide Point

Drafting the Wedge Full-Size

Up until now we've been using wedges with either a 4" or a 10" side to design the mandala. Now it's time to draft your wedge or wedges at actual size, then mark the pieces with the numbers and colors you'll need to sew your quilt together.

Spirals are sewn with foundation piecing. This means that the pattern is drawn full size on a foundation, which can be paper or a lightweight material like interfacing. The fabrics are sewn to the foundation, using the drawn lines as the seam lines. Because the lines on the paper guide the seams, it is not necessary to cut fabric accurately and match seam allowances. Once the spiral is sewn, a paper foundation is torn away, and a fabric foundation can be left in.

The first step to drawing the wedge full size is calculating the finished size of the quilt and the mandala. Decide how large your finished quilt will be, including background and borders. Figure the height and width of the background, the width of the border, the diameter (the distance across, or double the radius) and the radius (the measurement of the side of the wedge) of the finished mandala. The radius is the key measurement for enlarging the wedge.

Fussy Cuts and Quilt Size

Are there any fussy-cut fabrics in the design? If so, the size of the fussy cuts may determine the size of the whole quilt. In *Crest of the Crane* (page 120), the size of the entire quilt was determined by the size of the appliqué cranes.

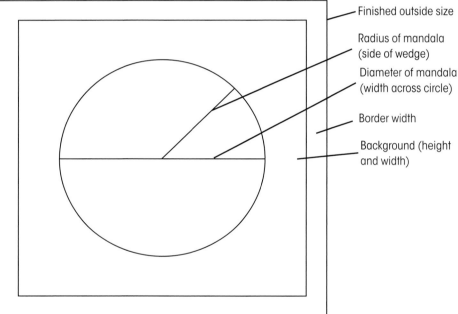

Finished outside size

Radius of mandala (side of wedge)

Diameter of mandala (width across circle)

Border width

Background (height and width)

Once you have these measurements, you can begin enlarging the wedge skeleton. It's okay to start by enlarging an empty wedge skeleton on a photocopy machine (see page 88), but then draft all the spirals in the wedge by hand, rather than simply enlarging the wedge puzzle. There are several reasons for this:

- Enlarging on a copy machine enlarges everything—including the thickness of the lines. Having thin, precise lines is essential to accurate sewing. Hand-drawing the spirals at full size avoids thickening lines as photocopying would.
- Drawing the wedges full size is the best way to make sure that all the points in your spirals meet precisely. (Drafting the wedge on a computer gives you these results as well.)

- Drafting the entire wedge as a single unit ensures that all the spirals in the wedge fit together precisely. If it fits on paper, it will fit in fabric.
- Drafting all the spirals side-by-side lets you work out smooth connections between them.
- Drafting all the spirals side-by-side makes sure that the colors in connecting flow forms are correct.

Once drafting is complete, the full-size wedge will be copied or printed onto regular paper for fabric-cutting templates and onto translucent paper or fabric for the foundations you'll use to sew the spirals (see page 95).

ENLARGING THE WEDGE SKELETON BY HAND

If you do not have a photocopier or computer available to enlarge your wedge skeleton, use this method to enlarge by hand. The wedge being enlarged here is from *Elizabeth* (page 128).

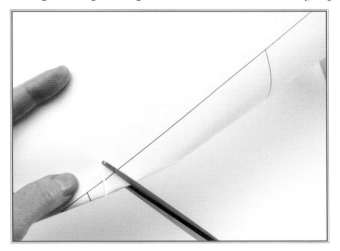

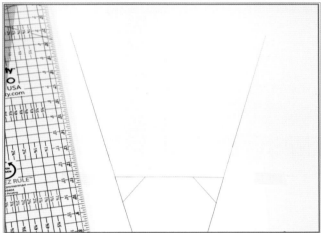

1 Tape a sheet of paper on your work surface. It should be large enough to contain the entire enlarged wedge.

Take a copy of your 10" wedge skeleton and cut a small opening just above the tip of the wedge. Tape the 10" wedge skeleton near the bottom of the large paper.

2 Using a long ruler and mechanical pencil, extend the sides of the wedge past the top of the 10" wedge to the length you want for the full-size wedge. Use the pencil alignment technique on pages 60–61. Keep the ruler precisely along the side of the 10" wedge so you don't alter the width of the wedge. If the width of the wedge changes, the wedges will not fit when you assemble the mandala.

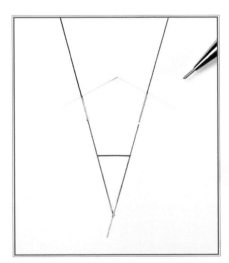

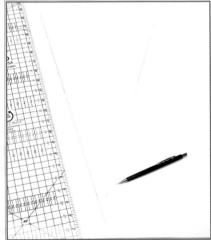

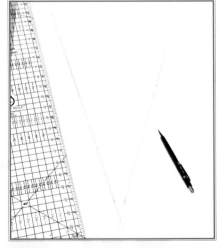

3 Extend the lines in Step 2 over the window near the point of the wedge.

4 Remove the 10" wedge from the larger paper. Using the sections of the line that appeared above the 10" wedge and in the window, complete the side lines and extend them down to make the point of the full-size wedge.

5 Draw the outside edge of the wedge. If the outside edge is the curved edge of a circle, print out the background template for that size circle from the CD that came with the book and use it as a template.

6 To fill in the skeleton lines on the full size wedge, measure the distance between the point of the wedge and each side node on the 10" wedge. Convert each measurement to its decimal equivalent using the chart on page 81. To get the enlargement ratio needed to convert the 10" wedge to the full-size wedge, take the length of the full-size radius and move the decimal place one place to the left. For example, if your full-size wedge has a 15" radius, the enlargement ratio is 1.5.

Multiply the measurements from the 10" wedge by the enlargement ratio. Convert the result back to inches. For example, if you have a side node 5" from the point of the 10" wedge and the enlargement ratio is 1.5, then 5" × 1.5 = 7½" which translates to a side node 7½" from the point of the full-size wedge. Measure and mark all of the nodes on the outside of the full-size wedge.

Using the nodes you marked, draw in the skeleton lines of the full-size wedge. If there are any nodes on internal skeleton lines, measure and mark them as described above. When all the lines of the enlarged skeleton are marked correctly, go over them again with a fine-tip black pen. Finally, make several copies of the enlarged wedge, so you'll have a master and some to experiment on.

ENLARGING THE WEDGE SKELETON ON A PHOTOCOPIER

To create a full-size wedge by photocopying, enlarge the 10" wedge (with the skeleton drawn in, but not the spirals) on a photocopy machine that can print on large paper, so the entire wedge will be on one sheet.

If copying on a single sheet isn't a possibility, enlarge the wedge skeleton in sections and assemble the sections. Draw match-up lines on the outside of the wedge and use these to align the photocopied sections.

To enlarge a 10" wedge to the size you want, just add a zero to the length of the desired radius. For example, if you want your full-size wedge to have a 22" radius, enlarge by 220 percent.

Make several copies of the enlarged wedge so you'll have a master copy and extra copies to experiment on.

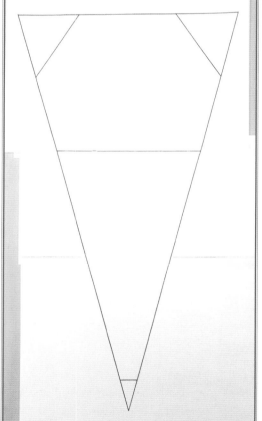

Photocopying, Printing and Accuracy

Although we think of printers and photocopiers as being accurate, the truth is that they can distort images. See pages 156–157 for information about photocopying, including how to avoid and/or compensate for distortion in copies of your foundations.

ENLARGING THE WEDGE ON A COMPUTER

ELECTRIC QUILT

The program Electric Quilt allows you to print a block at any size, no matter what size the original design is. If the quilt drawing is the actual size of the wedge you want, print at the size in the drawing. If you want to print the wedge at a different size than the drawing, set a custom size when printing. The controls for this are in the print dialogue box.

GRAPHIC DESIGN PROGRAMS

If you begin with a 10" wedge, you can use the "Scale" tool to enlarge it to the size desired. To calculate the percentage of enlargement, just add a zero to the length of the desired radius. For example, if you want your full-size wedge to have a 22" radius, enlarge 220 percent.

To enlarge manually, create a square with sides the same length as the desired radius of your wedge. If necessary, rotate the wedge so one side is parallel with the side of the box. Select the wedge and stretch it proportionally until the side of the wedge is the same length as the side of the box. Zoom in to check accuracy.

When working on a computer, do not enlarge files that are in .jpg format. Files in .jpg format enlarge the way photocopies do, so lines become thick and blurry. Also, .jpg files lose data every time they are revised. Graphic design program files, such as those created using Adobe Illustrator, are designed to accomodate enlargement, so they are fine.

Test the Fit

Once you have printed or copied templates, test that they fit together. Lay them together the way they'll fit in the wedge. If they don't fit exactly, lay them the way they are supposed to fit.

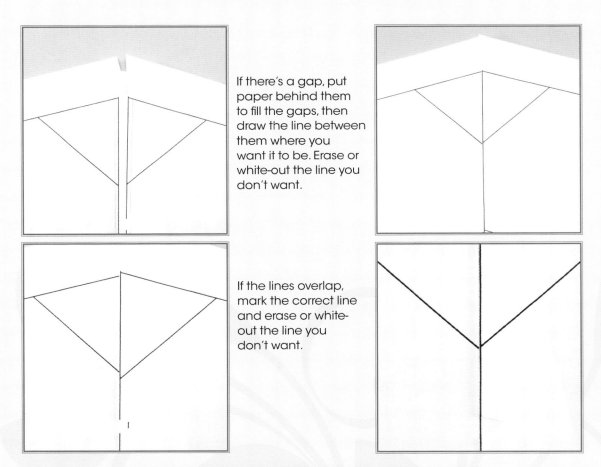

If there's a gap, put paper behind them to fill the gaps, then draw the line between them where you want it to be. Erase or white-out the line you don't want.

If the lines overlap, mark the correct line and erase or white-out the line you don't want.

Remember: If it fits on paper, it will fit in cloth. It's as simple as that.

DRAWING SPIRALS IN THE FULL-SIZE WEDGE

Once the full-size wedge skeleton is ready, the next step is drawing the spirals in each shape.

To begin, draw the first ring of every spiral in the wedge and set up the connections between all the spirals. It might be necessary in some cases to make adjustments in order for the spirals to connect smoothly. Here's what to look for:

- Where you had Nesting spirals in your wedge puzzle, now is the time to decide to switch to a Pinwheel or a hybrid spiral to create a stronger connection or to steer a curve (see page 79). If you're not sure which type of spiral would work better, draw the spiral both ways on two copies of the enlarged wedge skeleton to compare, then choose.
- Wherever two Nesting or two Baravelle spirals meet when spinning in opposite directions (usually a fan flow form), the two spirals on opposite sides of the line they share should share the same increment dot.
- Wherever two different types of spirals meet in any direction, you might need to make adjustments for the spokes to connect smoothly. Pages 89–91 show several simple adjustments for smoothly connecting spirals.

Any adjustment is okay if it helps the overall design flow smoothly. Two possibilities might be subdividing a corner, center or triangle, or cutting off a corner of a shape to add a spoke or make a smoother shape. You may find that small changes bring interesting new possibilities into your design.

As you set up smooth connections between the spirals in the wedge, remember to check for smooth connections between spirals from wedge to wedge where spirals create flow forms. Place a copy of the skeleton containing the first rings of the spirals along each side of the one you are drawing to check these connections.

Once you have set up the connections between the first rings of all the spirals, finish drafting the spirals inside each shape. As you build the spirals, watch for places where you want flowunders to appear (see page 47). Align the triangles of the sections that will "flow under" so that they appear to connect naturally from where they "pass under" to where they "reappear."

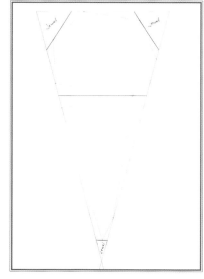

The full-size wedge with the first ring of each spiral drafted.

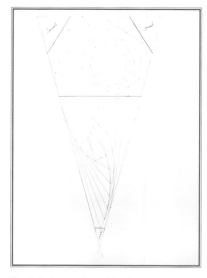

The full-size wedge with all spirals drafted in.

Tips for Spiral Selection

Nesting spirals: Use Nesting spirals wherever possible, because they are easier to draw and sew than Pinwheel spirals. They are less bulky at corners, so use a Nesting spiral (or a hybrid spiral) at the center of the mandala.

Pinwheel spirals: A Pinwheel spiral creates strong connections to all other spirals; they make thicker trunk flow forms than Nesting spirals. But avoid them in point/fan flow forms, because they pile up bulk along the seam. Use a Pinwheel or hybrid spiral if you want to steer the curve of a spoke or flow form.

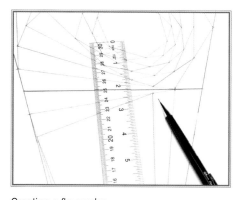

Creating a flowunder.

CONNECTING SPIRALS

Rough connections between spirals are most frequently caused by connecting different types of spirals that have different proportions. Sometimes they can also be caused by misalignments in the wedge skeleton. Here are situations to watch for and adjustments to smooth most connections. Ultimately, every mandala is unique and there are no rules, so be creative in finding what works for you.

WEDGE SKELETON ADJUSTMENTS
• Wherever two sides of any type of spirals connect, the sides of the shapes should be the same length and the corners of the shapes should match. If they don't, readjust the lines within the wedge skeleton so that they do. Check for matching side nodes between adjoining wedges too.

• If two corners of two shapes meet in the center of a single side of third shape, you have a T-joint. I recommend that you avoid these, but if you leave them in, see page 41 for tips on how to handle them.

NESTING SPIRAL CONNECTING TO A NESTING SPIRAL IN A FAN FLOW FORM

First, make sure the outer rings of the two spirals use the same increment dot (increment dots are marked in red in the illustrations below). This should have happened when you drew the first ring of every spiral in the wedge. While you're at it, also line up the increments on the next few rings to set up possible flowunders (marked by yellow lines in the illustrations below).

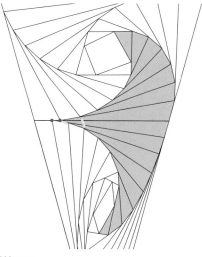

Wrong
Increments in the first ring of triangles don't match and triangles don't align for flowunder.

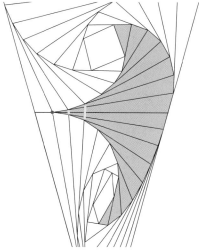

Right
Increments in the first ring of triangles do match. Increments in the next two rings align to set up a possible flowunder.

ANY TYPE OF SPIRAL, ANYWHERE YOU WANT
If there is a large corner or jewel between spirals, incorporate it into a connection, or subdivide that space to make a smooth connection. The grey area in this illustration shows how this was done in *Sultana* (page 144) to connect a Baravelle spiral at top to the Pinwheel spirals below. It ended up creating the red wraparound spokes that make the center of *Sultana* so interesting.

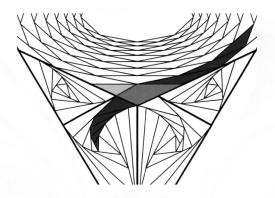

CONNECTING BARAVELLE SPIRALS TO OTHER TYPES OF SPIRALS

In Baravelle spirals, the increment dots always fall at the middle of the sides of the shape, so the triangles in the first ring of a Baravelle spiral don't align with the first ring of a different type of spiral.

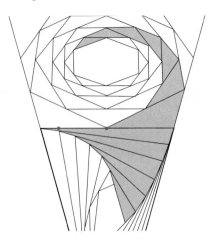

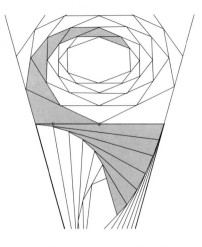

A fan connection between a Baravelle spiral (top) and a Pinwheel spiral (bottom) with increments that don't align.

A trunk connection between a Baravelle spiral (top) and a Pinwheel spiral (bottom) with increments that don't align.

For a smooth connection, draw the outer ring of a Baravelle spiral as a Nesting spiral on the connecting side, then change to a Baravelle spiral in the next ring toward the center. This lets you place the increment dot where it makes a smooth connection between spirals.

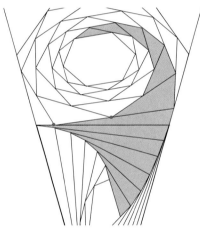

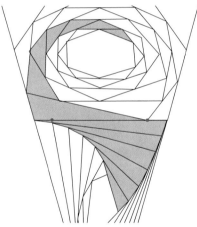

Fan Connection
The first ring of the Baravelle at right is drawn as a Nesting spiral for a smoother connection.

Trunk Connection
The first ring of this Baravelle is drawn as a Nesting spiral for a smoother connection.

You can make an even smoother connection by drawing the next few rings as Nesting spirals, too, adjusting the increment dots so that the Nesting spiral gradually changes to a Baravelle spiral as it moves toward the center of the spiral. This also lets you align increments for flowunders in fan connections (as shown by the yellow line in the illustration below left).

Fan Connection
The first four rings of this Baravelle spiral are drawn as a Nesting spiral, gradually adjusting to a Baravelle spiral, for the smoothest connection.

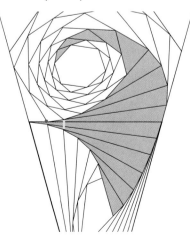

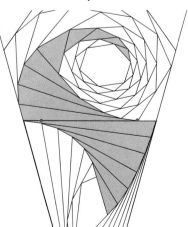

Trunk Connection
The first four rings of the Baravelle spiral at left are drawn as a Nesting spiral, gradually adjusting to a Baravelle spiral, for the smoothest connection.

Occasionally, starting a Baravelle spiral with one or more Pinwheel rings works even better than starting with a Nesting ring, particularly when connecting Baravelles to Point-to-Point spirals. This techniques can be used to connect different combinations of Nesting, Pinwheel and Point-to-Point spirals.

For more ways to combine different types of spirals, turn to Drawing Hybrid Spirals on page 82.

CONNECTING BARAVELLE SPIRALS TO BARAVELLE SPIRALS

In fan connections between Baravelle spirals, the spokes join halfway across the sides of the spirals, which often is adequate connection. But in trunk connections, the spokes don't connect at all. In this case, starting the Baravelle spirals with a Nesting or Pinwheel ring builds a strong, smooth connection.

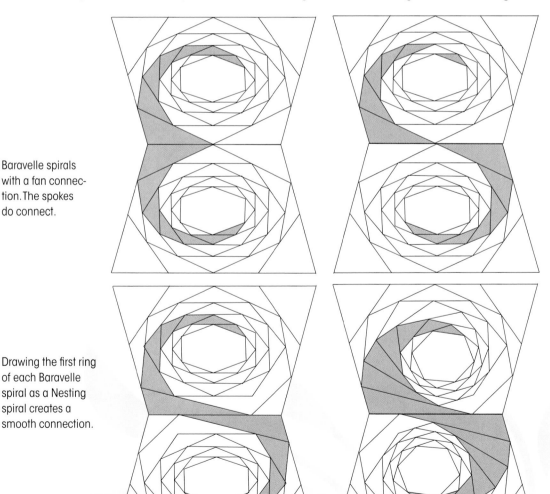

Baravelle spirals with a fan connection. The spokes do connect.

Baravelle spirals with a trunk connection. There is no contact between the spokes.

Drawing the first ring of each Baravelle spiral as a Nesting spiral creates a smooth connection.

Create an even smoother connection by drawing the first few rings as Nesting rings, gradually adjusting the increment dots to form Baravelle rings as you move toward the center.

LABELING SPIRALS

Now that your wedge is drafted, the next step is to label each piece for position and fabric. The master wedge contains the information you'll need to sew each spiral. Mark a master for each spiral in your design that has a different shape or color scheme.

Each spiral in your wedge puzzle has already been numbered or named in the wedge puzzle. Transfer those numbers or names to the centers of the spirals on the full-size wedge (without the C or X direction indicators). Note what type of spiral is used (Nesting, Pinwheel, Baravelle, Point-to-Point or Hybrid). Also label any jewels (shapes that do not contain spirals) in the wedge.

Next, label the spirals for sewing order and fabric. In each spiral, mark all the triangles in each ring with a letter, starting with A for the ring closest to the center, B for the next ring out, etc. Place all your color and number marks within ¼" from the base of each triangle. This helps you keep track of which side is the base where you cut the ¼" seam allowance, and the side you sew on. It also prevents you from positioning Type B triangles incorrectly (see pages 99–100). In addition, if you plan to leave the foundation in, the markings will fall under the seam allowances, preventing them from showing through light-colored fabrics.

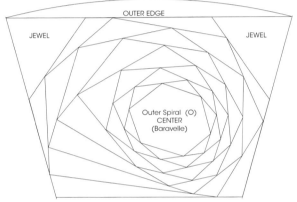

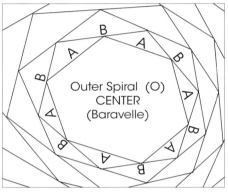

Next, number the triangles in order around Ring A. For Nesting and Baravelle spirals the numbers can go in either direction as long as you work in order. For Pinwheel and Point-to-Point spirals, number the triangles around the ring in the direction of the shortest side of the triangles. This will be the same direction as the spiral's direction of spin: If the spiral spins clockwise, the numbers get higher as you go clockwise around the ring, and vice versa. For hybrid spirals (one or more spokes is Nesting and the others are Pinwheel), start at the triangle in a Nesting spoke, then work in the direction of the shortest side of the Pinwheel triangles.

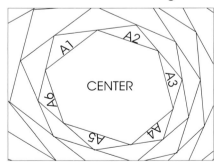

Nesting and Baravelle spirals can be numbered in either direction.

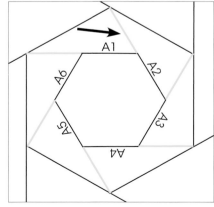

The numbering for Pinwheel and Point-to-Point spirals should go toward the shortest side of the triangle (marked in yellow above).

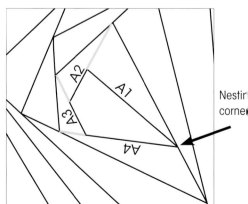

The numbering for hybrid spirals should start at the Nesting triangle and move toward the shortest side of the other triangles (marked in yellow above).

Now, working from the center out, label all the triangles in each spoke with the same number as the A triangle in that spoke: 1 for all triangles in the spoke beginning with A1, 2 for all triangles in the spoke beginning with A2, etc. Each triangle now has a unique number/letter combination that indicates its position in the spiral—A1, B1, C1, etc. If you have a differently colored version of the wedge or any of the spirals, make a copy for each version now.

Next, label each triangle of each spiral with the name and version (if applicable) of that spiral. This will avoid getting pieces of different spirals mixed up if you cut fabric for all of the spirals at the same time, since every spiral has an A1, A2, A3, etc. It's a good idea, at least the first time you make a mandala, to cut and sew only one group of the same spiral at a time to avoid mix-ups.

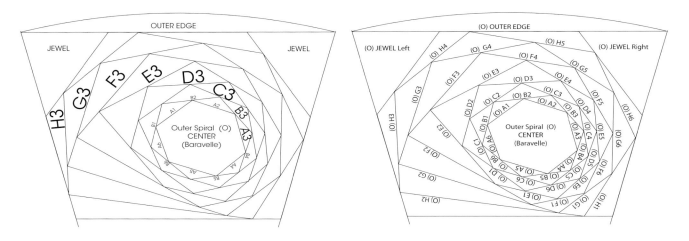

Finally, in each triangle of each spiral write the color of the fabric for that triangle. Also mark any areas that will contain fussy cuts, including any marks you might need for positioning the fussy cut. Write the name rather than marking with a colored marker so the color won't be lost on a black-and-white photocopy. (Don't use numbers for colors—too many different numbers can become confusing.)

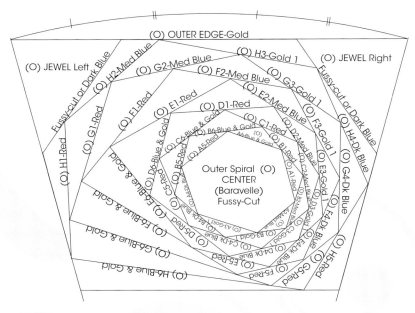

When all the markings are complete, make a copy of your master template(s) on white paper. Keep the original to refer to as you assemble your mandala. The copy will be cut up for cutting templates.

COPYING SPIRALS FOR FOUNDATIONS

The easiest way to make foundations from the master wedge is to simply photocopy them onto translucent foundation material. For quilts that are smaller than bed size, most wedges will have a radius of 24" or less. Depending on the number of shapes in the wedge, most of the individual spirals in the wedge will probably fit either on a single 8½" × 11" sheet of paper, or two sheets joined together. In the latter case, simply draw a matching line on either side of the spiral (see page 86), then photocopy it in pieces. Join the pieces for a complete foundation.

I use foundation materials that come in 8½" × 11" sheets because they can go through a printer or photocopier. If you're using a regular photocopy machine or laser printer, use translucent foundation paper; if you're using an inkjet printer, you can use either translucent paper or nonwoven foundation sheets. Personally, I prefer an inkjet printer for two reasons: First, the ink absorbs into the paper more, so it is easier to see from the back side. Second, since photocopiers fuse the toner to the paper with heat, sometimes a hot iron will remove toner from foundation paper.

In case the printer or photocopier has some distortion, try to print or copy each portion of the wedge in the same direction on the printer or copier so any distortion will all happen in the same direction. That said, remember that fabric is flexible—it can ease and stretch, so if there is under ⅛" distortion in the foundations, you can likely ease it when putting the spirals and the wedges together. It's not a bad idea to check the fit of all the foundations again, before beginning to sew the spirals. (See page 156 for more about printing and distortion.)

Another way to transfer the wedge to the foundation is to trace the master onto a piece of translucent material large enough to hold the entire wedge. Tape, pin or staple the foundation material over the master wedge. Trace by hand all the markings from the master wedge to the foundation. Make as many foundations as there are wedges in your mandala. Then, cut apart the individual spirals for piecing. One advantage of this method is that you know every shape of the wedge fits together perfectly.

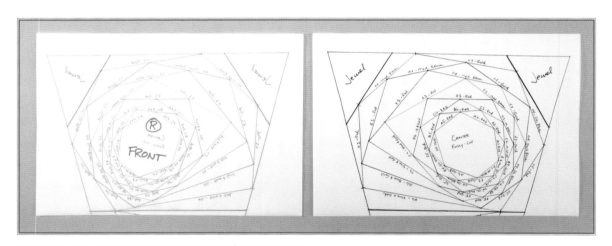

If there are both original and reverse versions of a spiral in your design, simply make original orientation copies on the translucent foundation, then turn the copy over and mark the back "Reverse." Mark this in the center of the spiral, where you'll place the first piece of fabric so you get the fabric on the correct side from the start.

Foundation Materials

I consider translucent foundation material essential for foundation piecing for one simple reason: You can see through it. Traditional methods of paper piecing involve drawing the design on opaque paper, then placing fabric on the back. This presents two problems: First, you can't see the lines from the back; and second, the design that you sew is the mirror image of the design that you drew, which can be really confusing. Translucent foundation lets you see the lines from both sides. So, you place the fabric on the front of the foundation and the design doesn't get reversed. Translucent foundation also makes the design process easier, because all you need to do to create a mirror image of a spiral is simply turn the foundation over and mark the back "Reverse."

There is a wide variety of translucent foundation materials on the market. Most come in 8½" × 11" sheets that can pass easily through a photocopier or printer. I use either translucent foundation paper or nonwoven foundation sheets, depending on the type of project I'm working on.

Translucent foundation paper can be photocopied, printed on with an inkjet or laser printer, and written on by hand. It must be removed after piecing. Nonwoven foundation sheets can be printed on an inkjet printer and written on by hand. They can be left in after piecing or removed. Some people don't like removing a paper foundation after piecing; if that's you, use a nonwoven foundation that can be left in the finished quilt. Some people like rinse-away foundations; I don't because I don't want to wash, wet, press and block all the seams in a mandala!

When selecting a foundation for your project, it should have these characteristics:

- You can see the lines from both sides of the material.
- You can mark the design easily on the material—print on it, photocopy on it or write on it.
- The markings remain permanent on the material through washing and ironing.
- The material holds up to being folded, pressed and scrunched through a sewing machine numerous times.
- The material can be easily removed or safely left in your project.
- If the material is being left in, it should not shrink, clump, shred or melt, and it needs to be light enough to quilt through.

What not to use:

- Don't mix different types of foundation—different materials may respond to washing, heat and sewing tension differently, and you could end up with spirals that have changed size and don't fit together.
- Don't use vellum paper from the stationery store—it curls and becomes brittle when ironed. If you do use it, cold-press with a seam roller or a wooden presser (see page 100).
- Stay away from art store tracing paper—it's not strong enough to hold up to manipulation. Also, like vellum, it can curl and become brittle when ironed.
- Newsprint is good for sketching and working out ideas, but not for sewing. It is not translucent and it is also not strong enough to hold up to manipulation.

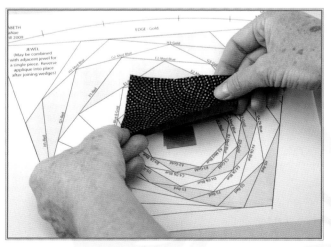

Using translucent foundation paper makes it easy to place the fabrics on the design from the front without reversing the design.

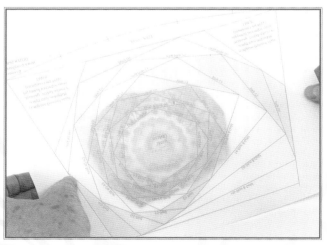

The design is still visible on the back of the translucent foundation material, which makes it easy to sew or reverse a template.

Cutting Fabric for Spirals

The last step before you get to start sewing (yes, we're almost there!) is cutting your fabrics. Begin with calculating yardage, then prepare the cutting templates, and, finally, cut the fabric.

To cut the fabrics for your spirals, you will need the following items:
- Paper scissors
- Rotary cutter, ruler and mat
- Double-sided tape (the permanent kind, not the removable kind)
- Straight pins, safety pins or binder clips

CALCULATING YARDAGE

Here are two ways to figure out how much fabric you'll need for your mandala. One method uses the cutting templates to measure fabric; the other estimates an amount based on the size of the finished mandala.

THE TEMPLATE METHOD

When you prepared your foundations, you made a white paper copy of each foundation to cut up for cutting templates. Cut apart these cutting templates and lay them out on paper or fabric as you would on the fabrics for your mandala (see cutting fabric instructions on pages 97-99). Measure the amount of each fabric needed for one copy of each spiral, then multiply this amount by how many copies of that spiral are in your mandala.

THE ESTIMATING METHOD

To begin, measure the mandala in inches and multiply width by height. (For a circle, the width and height are the same. For an oval, the numbers will be different.) This gives you the area of the finished mandala in square inches, plus a bit more. For example, if your mandala is 40" × 40", the area of the full mandala is 1600 square inches (40" × 40" = 1600). Next, convert the area of the mandala from inches to yards. In a yard of fabric there are 1440 square inches of fabric (36" × 40" = 1440 square inches). Divide the number of square inches in your mandala by 1440: for our example this would mean dividing

1600 by 1440, which is 1.1 yards (1600 / 1440 = 1.1). After that, multiply the area of the mandala in yards by 3 to add additional fabric for cutting rectangular strips and for seam allowances. This gives you the total yardage you'll need to create your mandala. For our example, with an area of 1.1 yards, we'll need 3.3 yards of fabric (1.1 x 3 = 3.3).

Now count the number of different fabrics in your mandala. Divide the total yardage needed by the number of fabrics. This gives you the average amount you'll need of each fabric. Let's say there are 10 fabrics, so the 3.3 yards of fabric will be divided by 10, giving us an average of .33 yards per fabric (3.3 / 10 = .33). Use the chart above to convert this decimal to a fraction for measuring fabric. For our example, which requires .33 yards of fabric per color, we'll buy ⅜ yard of fabric on average. From there, look at how much of each fabric is in the design. For fabrics that are used a lot more or less than others, increase or decreasethe amount. Of course, it's always a good idea to buy a little extra for insurance (and for stash-building).

TIP

If you don't have enough of a fabric for the whole mandala (or if you're not sure), cut one spiral (all copies) at a time. If the fabric appears in another area of the design but you run out, the replacement fabric will be consistent in the other areas. If you have to change fabric among copies of the same spiral, arrange the replacement fabric symmetrically around the mandala, so the difference in fabrics becomes a logical part of the design.

BACKGROUND

If you plan to appliqué the mandala over a background, multiply the width by the height of the background area and add seam allowances, then convert the total to yards, using the chart on page 96.

If you plan to piece the background, use the same measurements as above, and you'll have some left over. If you want a more exact measurement, print the appropriate background templates from the CD and physically lay them out to measure the amount of fabric you'll need.

BORDERS

If the borders for your quilt are pieced, use either the Estimating Method or the Template Method to calculate yardage.

For solid borders, multiply the width of the border strip plus its seam allowances by the length of the border strip, then multiply that number by the number of sides on your quilt. For mitered corners, make all strips the full length of each side. If you don't want to piece borders, buy fabric the length of the border strip.

FUSSY CUTTING

For fussy cutting, count how many copies of a motif you need. Rather than calculate yardage, look at fabric when you are at the store and buy the number of repetitions of the motif that you need. Keep in mind that if two motifs are so close together that cutting one with seam allowances will cut into the other, you will need twice as many motifs to end up with the correct number.

STRIPES, GEOMETRICS AND OTHER DIRECTIONAL PRINTS

Lay out cutting templates based on how you plan to position these prints in the design, then physically measure the amount of fabric you'll need.

PREPARING THE CUTTING TEMPLATES

Handle your templates carefully and keep them organized now—this will save you a lot of time and frustration down the road!

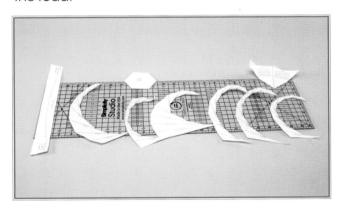
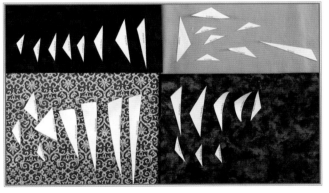

1 On the cutting template copy of the master wedge, place strips of double-sided tape across the entire back of the spirals, ⅛"–¼" apart. (Don't stretch the tape as you stick it down, or it will cause the templates to pucker. If you do get a pucker, slit the tape behind it with a small pair of scissors or a seam ripper.)

Cut apart the spirals into individual spokes, centers and jewels (if any). I cut this way because more often than not, spokes are primarily one fabric; cutting this way helps keep the templates organized by fabric. I recommend sticking the pieces to a large ruler to keep them organized and to keep them from sticking to each other, but let the templates hang over the edge so they are easy to pull off.

2 Gather all the fabrics for the spirals. Square off one cut edge of each fabric and lay the fabrics out on your work surface. Cut each spoke of the spiral into its separate triangles and center. As you do, stick each template to its corresponding fabric.

CUTTING FABRIC STRIPS

When cutting fabric for the triangles that make up your spirals, cut rectangular strips. These strips will be trimmed down to triangles after they are sewn to the foundation. This does waste some fabric, but the advantages are worth it:

- Cutting strips is faster and easier than cutting individual triangles.
- If you leave the fabric in strips and cut off lengths as you sew, small pieces won't get lost.
- You'll never accidentally cut a triangle backwards, because a rectangle fits either a "left" or a "right" triangle.
- If you scoot the fabric too far to the left or right when sewing it, you will still have adequate height for a seam allowance, so you won't have to undo and resew.
- The edges of your spokes will be smoother because the extra fabric gives you a handle

to grasp when pressing, so you'll press precisely on the seam line.

- The extra fabric makes small pieces easier to handle.
- On long, narrow triangles, the extra fabric provides stability to keep the points from wobbling.

If you cut all of the fabric for all of the spirals in the wedge at the same time before you start cutting, be sure that the individual pieces of the spirals are all marked to indicate which spiral they go in. Otherwise, you'll end up with several pieces with the same number and no way to tell which spiral they belong to! You might find it easier at first to cut and sew multiples of only one spiral at a time.

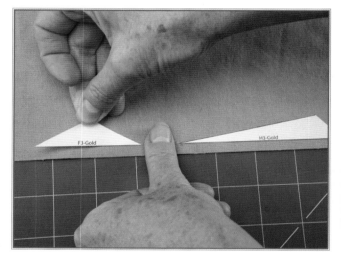

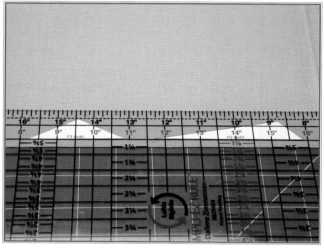

1 Working with one fabric at a time, lay the fabric on the cutting mat with the squared edge toward you. The fabric can be folded in layers. (Be careful that the templates don't fall off as you handle the fabric.)

Lay the cutting templates with their bases ¼" from the cut edge and the triangles ½" apart—a thumb width is just right. Group the templates so that templates of the same height are on the same strip.

2 Place the rotary cutting ruler over the templates, with the edge ¼" above the peak of the highest triangle in the row. (Don't cut pieces larger than this; the excess fabric gets in the way when sewing.) Keep the ruler parallel with the cut edge of the fabric.

TIP

If you really hate to waste any fabric, go to http://spiromandalas.wordpress.com for a fun, easy project to make with the cutaway scraps when you finish the mandala.

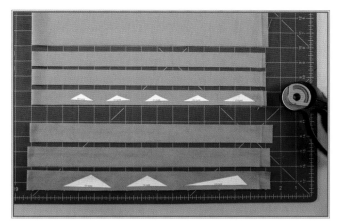

3 Cut a strip across the width of the fabric (WOF). Then, cut enough additional strips of the same width so you have one layer of fabric for each copy of this spiral. For example, if you have 6 copies of this spiral, cut enough strips to have 6 layers of fabric. (In this example, the fabric is 2 layers thick, so 3 strips make 6 layers.)

4 As you cut strips, pin or clip each group together with the templates on top. Leave the templates on the fabrics and the fabrics in strips. (I hang them on my design wall this way.) Snip off a stack of fabric for each template as you are ready to sew that piece. Or, to speed up sewing, cut the long strips down to the triangle-size pieces all at once and group the pieces by ring and spiral before beginning.

TIP

Arrange the templates alphabetically on the strips of fabric–Spiral 1 A's, B's and C's; Spiral 2 A's, B's and C's, etc. Then, you can cut the pieces off as you need them without having to move the templates.

If fabric is tight . . .

It is possible to cut templates to shape, but do it only if you need to conserve fabric. Be extra careful to cut any reverse versions of templates correctly, otherwise you might waste precious fabric on mistakes.

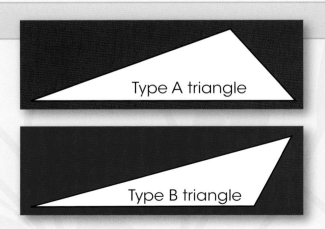

Type A and Type B Triangles

The base is not always the longest side of a triangle. In Type A triangles (top right), the longest side is the base, but in Type B triangles (bottom right), the base is the mid-length side and the peak extends past the base. Labeling the triangles along the base helps to distinguish Type A triangles from Type B triangles. The ¼" seam allowance should always be on the base side of the triangle as shown above, because this is the edge that aligns with the trimmed seam allowance of the previous ring, and the edge where you sew.

Type A triangle

Type B triangle

99

Tools and Techniques for Sewing Spirals

TOOLS FOR SEWING SPIRALS

In addition to basic sewing tools you will need:

- A center-slot or open-toe sewing machine foot—whatever gives you a clear view of the lines on the foundation
- Masking tape or Painter's tape, 1" wide
- Seam roller for quick and easy pressing—optional, but very useful
- Two highlighter pens or light-colored fabric pens in different colors
- Add-a-Quarter tool (Add-an-Eighth for small areas) and a piece of cardstock
- Rotary cutter and mat—a small one you can use at the sewing machine is nice

SEWING MACHINE SET-UP

I recommend the following settings for sewing spirals:

Tension: Use a normal tension that lets the threads cross between the layers of fabric, not on the back or the front. If you're using removable foundation, the stitches will be looser when the foundation is gone.

Stitch Length: Set your stitch length to about 20 stitches per inch for removable foundation; for leave-in foundation, I advise about 15 stitches per inch. Shorter stitches are tighter, less likely to come undone at the ends of your seams and less likely to pull out when you remove foundation material.

Needle: Use a 80/12 or 70/10 needle when sewing spirals. Have several needles on hand—sewing through paper dulls needles more quickly than sewing fabric. Use a finer needle with a finer thread.

Thread: Use fine cotton or silk thread that will add a minimum of bulk to seams—I recommend 50-weight thread or finer. Select a good quality, strong thread and use a color that will blend into the fabric.

Foot: Use a foot that allows you a clear view of the foundation. A center mark or slot helps you align the needle with the lines on the foundation. Check the needle position to make sure it aligns with the mark on the foot.

TIP

A seam roller is one of my favorite tools. It makes a firm, clean fold and is quick and easy to use right at the sewing machine. Get one with a barrel-shaped (not cylindrical) roller (see Resources, page 157).

Positioning Fabric on the Foundation

- You cut your fabric strips with a ¼" seam allowance along the base of each triangle. As you sew, you'll do what I call a "Next Step Trim" (see pages 102–103) that sets up the same ¼" seam allowance on pieces you have sewn into place. To position fabric, just align the long edges of fabric strips with the trimmed pieces already sewn on the foundation (see pages 104-105).

- As you work, get in the habit of positioning fabric from tip to peak of the triangle. This will help you avoid cutting off the peak of Type B triangles.

- Rather than pins, I use painter's tape to hold fabric in position for stitching. Buy the stickiest type.

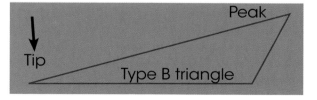

Right

Peak

Tip

Type B triangle

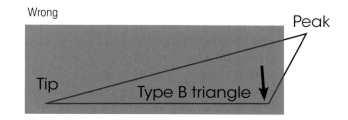

Wrong

Peak

Tip

Type B triangle

STITCHING TECHNIQUES

- After positioning the fabric on the front of the foundation, turn the foundation and fabric over and stitch along the seam line on the back of the foundation. This lets you see the seam line and stitch on it precisely.
- Begin and end one or two stitches beyond the ends of the seam line. This will tuck the thread ends under the next piece of fabric. Do not backstitch. Backstitching adds bulk, which will complicate joining spirals and wedges later on.
- If the lines on the foundation are wider than the thread, decide before you start sewing whether you will stitch on the inside edge or the outside edge of the line, and follow this decision through the whole quilt. This will help keep your points sharp and all your spirals the right size.
- Don't try to correct a mistake by adjusting other seam lines around it. Remove the incorrect seam and restitch. All the lines of a spiral are interrelated, so stitching off line on one seam will affect all the triangles and rings beyond it.

CROSSING INTERSECTIONS

As you add rings to the spiral, the new seams will cross the previously sewn corners of the prior ring of triangles. It is very important that you cross these intersections correctly so the corners of the triangles meet precisely and the edges of the spokes are smooth. Pay close attention to these examples so you know what to do and what to avoid.

MANAGING BULK

The areas around narrow points will become bulky as the layers of fabric grow. The bulk may cause the fabric to slip out from under the sewing machine foot, the layers of fabric to slip out of alignment or seam lines to become crooked. Here are several solutions to this problem:

- Start sewing at the bulkiest part of the seam so the foot slides off the bulk instead of onto it.
- Use "Good-to-the-Last-Stitch Pinning" (see page 110).
- Stitch slowly and hold the fabric under the foot with the tip of a seam ripper, bamboo skewer or stiletto.
- Lighten the pressure on the foot. Some sewing machine feet have a button you can press to stabilize the foot over thick areas to prevent slipping. Some newer sewing machines have a sensor that does this automatically.

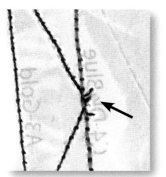 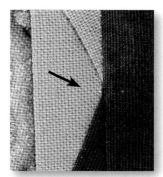

Right: Stitch so that the needle/thread just touches the inside of the threads of the previous intersection.

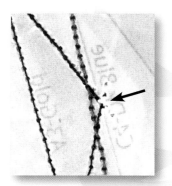  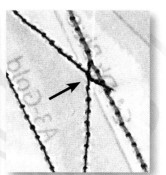 

Wrong: If you stitch inside the intersection of stitching lines, the corners of the triangles will not meet.

Wrong: If you stitch outside the intersection of stitching lines, the triangles will overlap, creating a hook on the edge of the spoke.

SET THE SPIRAL CENTER

All spirals are constructed by sewing rings of triangles from center to edge. Though the order of sewing is a bit different for Nesting and Baravelle spirals than for Pinwheel and Point-to-Point spirals, the first step for all spirals—setting the center—is the same.

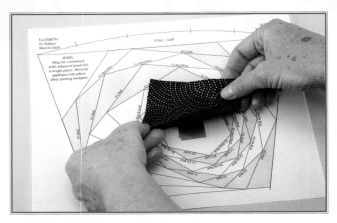

Put a dot of fabric glue or a rolled piece of Painter's tape on the foundation in the center of the spiral. (You'll remove the tape later, after completing the spiral, so don't use double-sided tape here—it's easy to forget and difficult to remove.)

If the center is not pieced or fussy cut, simply place the center fabric face up over the center area on the front of the foundation.

If the center is pieced or fussy cut, place the fabric face down on your work surface. Turn the foundation face down and float it over the center until it is positioned correctly, then stick it down.

Do a next step trim around the center to trim the fabric to size and set up the seam allowance for the first ring of triangles (see below).

NEXT STEP TRIM

As you sew the spiral, you'll do a next step trim after sewing all of the pieces of fabric in each ring of triangles. A next step trim cuts the rectangular strips of fabric down to the shapes of the center and the triangles in the spiral. At the same time, it sets up the correct seam allowance for the next ring of triangles.

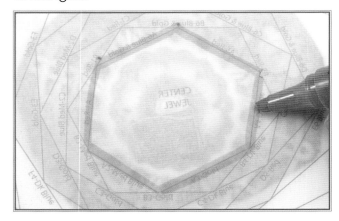

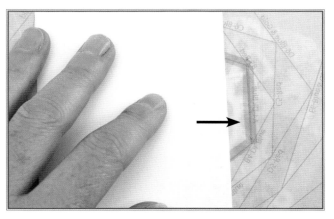

1 To start a spiral, do a next step trim around the center. Place the foundation fabric side down. On the foundation side, highlight the seam lines that surround the center.

2 Place a card along the highlighted line. (This is the bottom of the A triangles.)

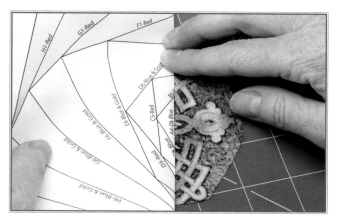

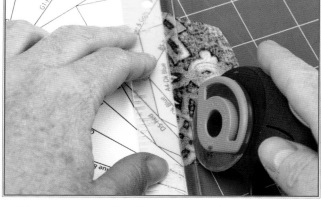

3 Fold the foundation back over the card. The fabric should extend beyond the folded edge of the foundation.

4 Place the Add-a-Quarter or Add-an-Eighth tool along the edge of the folded foundation. Trim the excess fabric with the rotary cutter.

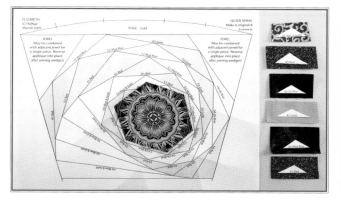

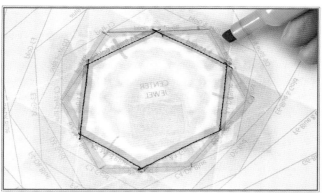

5 Repeat Steps 2–4 on each side of the shape. Once the trimming is complete, the center piece or the ring of triangles is cut to size with a ¼" (or ⅛") seam allowance on each side. Sew the fabric for the next ring of triangles into place.

6 To begin the next step trim on the newly added ring of triangles, highlight the foundation along the seam line you're going to sew for the next ring of triangles. Use a different color from the previous ring. Then, repeat Steps 2–5. For example, if you just sewed the A ring, you'll highlight and trim the bottom of the B triangles.

TIP

In a next step trim, the highlighted ring for Nesting and Baravelle spirals is an enclosed shape (shown throughout this demonstration). Point-to-Point and Pinwheel spirals (at right) are different: they have lines that stick out from the shape.

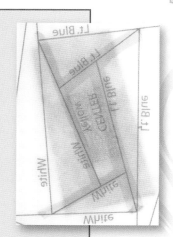

Watch Out!

As you work through the rings of the spiral, be careful not to fold back the foundation along the line of stitching that you just sewed. If you do, you will cut off all the pieces you just sewed on, and you will have to recut and resew all the cut-off pieces. (I call this mistake a "hack-and-howl.") This is why I recommend a different color highlighter on the next line—to make the new line look different. If a hack-and-howl happens to you, give yourself a chocolate break to calm down before attempting to fix it!

103

SEWING NESTING AND BARAVELLE SPIRALS

With Nesting and Baravelle spirals, the order you sew the pieces of fabric in each ring doesn't matter, because the triangles don't overlap like they do in Pinwheel and Point-to-Point spirals. You can sew one piece at a time, or, for faster sewing, sew two or more pieces in the same step, as long as they are not next to each other in the ring. The instructions here show how to sew multiple pieces of fabric at the same time.

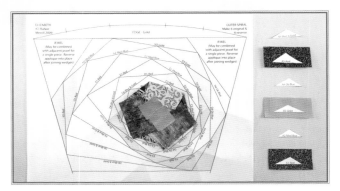

1 Position the center fabric (see page 102) on the correct side of the foundation. Do a next step trim around the center (see pages 102–103).

Position fabrics for the odd-numbered triangles face down over the center fabric, aligning the long edges of the fabric strips with the edge of center. If the spiral has an uneven number of sides, leave off the fabric for the highest-numbered triangle in this step. After completing Step 4, repeat Steps 2–4 for the last odd-numbered triangle.

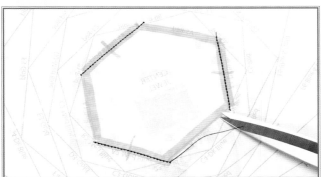

2 Turn the foundation over and stitch from the back along the seam line for each odd-numbered triangle. Begin and end the seam 2 or 3 stitches beyond each end of the line. Trim all threads on the back so you don't confuse them with lines on the foundation.

Flip the foundation right side up and trim threads. Press back the newly attached pieces from the seam line. (See below.)

Press Seams As You Go

As you sew pieces of fabric into place, press back each strip before sewing another piece of fabric over it. Follow these easy steps for perfect pressing.

1 Hold onto the extra fabric of the rectangular strip and gently tug the fabric back until you can see the stitches. This is critical for having smooth edges on the spokes of the spiral. Press the fabric precisely along the seam. Whenever you press a spiral with an iron, move the iron from the center of the spiral toward the edge so the fabric is pressed back along the seam.

2 If necessary, pin or tape the loose edge of the pressed fabric to the foundation to prevent it from slipping back over the seam line or getting caught in another seam.

If you see "hooks" on the edges of your spokes, the most likely reason is that the fabric is folded over the seam line. To avoid hooks, make sure to pull the fabric all the way back to the seam line when pressing.

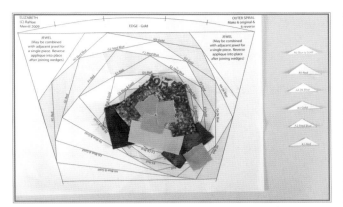

3 Position the fabric for the even-numbered triangles face down on the front of the foundation. Tape the pieces of fabric into position.

4 Following the instructions in Step 2, sew and press the even-numbered triangles.

If the spiral has an uneven number of sides, repeat Steps 2–4 now for the last odd-numbered piece of fabric.

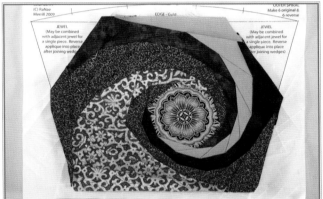

5 Do a next step trim to remove excess fabric and set up the seam allowance for the next ring of triangles (see page 102). To avoid confusion, highlight the next seam line with a different color than the previous one.

6 Repeat Steps 2–5 for each ring of triangles, moving out from the center. Carefully follow the color placements marked on the foundation. As you add rings, you will see the spokes grow and curve.

When you complete the spiral, trim ¼" beyond the outside line of the spiral for a seam allowance. Do not remove the foundation.

If the foundation will remain in the quilt, remove the tape in the center of the spiral by tearing away the center of the foundation.

Handling Small Pieces

A challenge that beginners face when sewing spirals is that you begin with the smallest pieces at the center, just when you're first learning. With all those small pieces, it may seem like a spiral will take forever to sew. But take heart—the process becomes easier and faster. To make it as painless as possible, sew the largest spirals in your design first to get familiar with the process. Use pieces of fabric large enough to handle comfortably.

One at a Time

Even if you are sewing more than one piece of fabric at the same time, in small areas such as a center it may be necessary to sew one strip of fabric at a time to avoid overlapping.

TIP

Sewing spirals requires concentration. To prevent mistakes, try to avoid distractions and sew at times when you are not tired. Take breaks often to refresh yourself and stay alert.

SEWING PINWHEEL AND POINT-TO-POINT SPIRALS

In Pinwheel and Point-to-Point spirals, each triangle overlaps the triangle next to it in the ring. Because of this, the pieces of fabric must be sewn one at a time in order around the ring. Pinwheel and Point-to-Point Spirals usually require partial seam piecing—the end of the first piece of fabric is left unsewn until the last piece is in place.

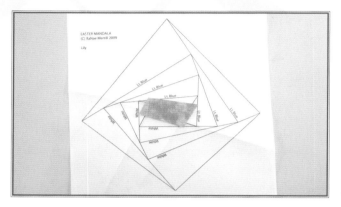

1 Position the center fabric (see page 102). Do a next step trim around the center to shape it and set up seam allowances for Ring A (see pages 102–103). Remember, if you turned the foundations for Reverse versions, the side marked "Reverse" is now the front.

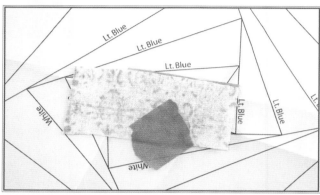

2 Position the fabric for the first triangle face down on the front of the foundation. Align the long edge with the trimmed edge of the center. Tape it into position, avoiding the seam line.

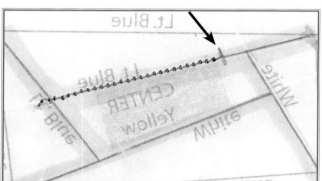

3 Turn the foundation over and stitch on the back part way along the seam line from the wide end toward the narrow tip of the triangle but leave the narrow tip of the triangle unsewn. Stop at least ¼" before the seam line of the last triangle. This is a partial seam. You'll come back and finish it later.

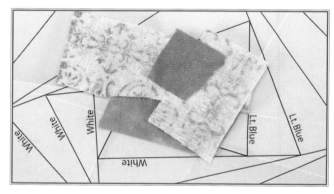

4 Flip the newly-added fabric right side up and press it back from seam line (see page 104). If necessary, tape the loose edge into position.

Working around the ring in numerical order, position the next piece of fabric face down on the front of the foundation, aligning the long edge with the trimmed edge of the center or previous ring. Tape it into place. (The next piece of fabric is always the one that covers the shortest side of the triangle you just sewed.)

TIP

In Pinwheel or Point-to-Point spirals, you might need to trim a bit of excess fabric from a seam before sewing a piece of fabric over the previous one. Just snip these with scissors as you find them (it will be apparent where and when needed).

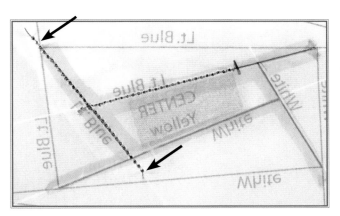

5 Turn the foundation over and stitch on the back all the way along the seam line of the piece just added.

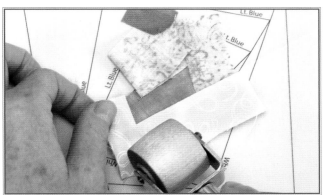

6 Flip the fabric right side up and press it back from the seam line. If necessary, tape the loose edge of fabric into position.

Repeat Steps 4–5, adding triangles around the ring in order until the ring is complete. When sewing the last strip into place, pin the loose end of the first strip out of the way so it doesn't catch in the last seam. Sew the last seam, then flip and press back the last strip of fabric.

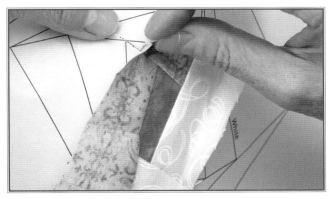

7 Locate the seam between the first and second triangles in the ring (the one that crosses the short side of the first triangle). Grasp all layers of fabric and tear the seam free from the foundation without unstitching it.

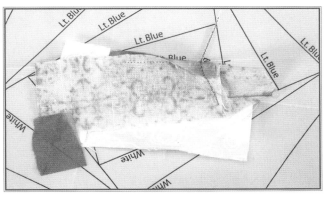

8 Unfold the first strip of fabric so it lays flat, face down, with the seam open. Align the loose edge of the fabric with the trimmed edge of the center or previous ring. (It will overlap the last strip of fabric in the ring and will not align with its edge.) Tape or pin it securely in position.

TIP

If the fabrics in the first and last triangles are the same, there's no need for a partial seam. Sew the full seam on the first triangle, then sew the last triangle over the first. The fabric will hide the cut-off tip.

TIP

If the length of the partial seam is quite short, skip Steps 7-10. Just hold the piece of fabric in place for now with a pin or a touch of fabric glue, then catch it in the seam of the next ring. Later, the quilting will close the gap.

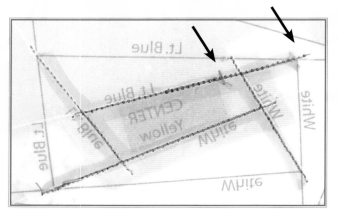

9 Turn to the foundation side and finish stitching the seam for the first triangle.

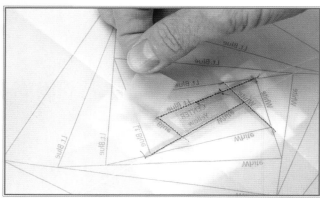

10 Put a piece of transparent tape over the tear in the foundation. Press the first strip of fabric into position. Pin the torn-out seam precisely back over its seam line through the transparent tape.

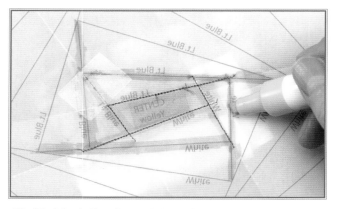

11 Mark the foundation for the next step trim. To avoid confusion, highlight the next seam line with a different color than the previous one.

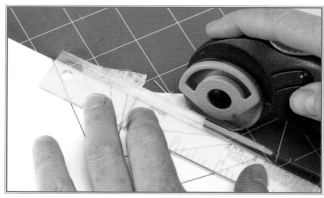

12 Do a next step trim to remove excess fabric and set up the seam allowance for the next ring of triangles.

13 Repeat the steps above for each ring of triangles, moving out from the center. Carefully follow the color placements marked on the foundation. As you add rings to the spiral, you will see the spokes grow and curve.

When you complete the spiral, trim ¼" beyond the outside line of the spiral for a seam allowance to join the spirals. Do not remove the foundation.

If you are using foundation material that will remain in the quilt, remove the tape in the center of the spiral by tearing away only the center of the foundation.

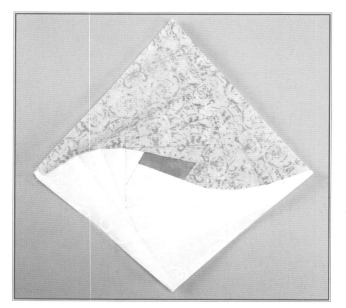

Assembling the Mandala

After all the individual spirals are sewn, join the spirals into wedges, and the wedges into a circular mandala. Leave in the foundations during assembly—the markings are essential for joining the spirals and wedges.

PINNING TECHNIQUES

I don't use pins when sewing spirals, but I do use them when joining spirals together. Combine the two techniques below for perfectly aligned points and seams.

ACUPOINT PINNING

Begin with Acupoint pinning for perfectly matched points.

1 Working from the side you will sew from, stick a pin precisely through both points you want to match.

2 Pinch the fabric/foundations together on the shaft of the pin.

3 Stick another pin diagonally and almost flat through all of the pinned layers, entering the fabric precisely at the base of the first pin. Bend the foundation just enough to bring the pin back up through the fabric as far from the entry point as possible. While you are doing this, the first pin prevents the layers from shifting. Remove the first pin.

When you sew, put the needle down precisely at the entry point of the second pin (remove it just before you take the stitch) and the points will match.

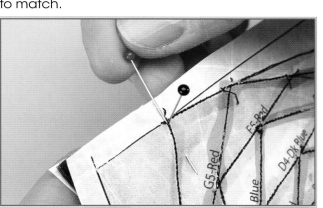

"Y" Seams

Don't let "Y" seams scare you. Simply match corner points and seam lines on the foundations using these pinning techniques. Sew precisely to the pinned intersection point, then backstitch a few stitches to prevent them from pulling loose when you sew the other seams. Do this on all three seams, and they'll fall together perfectly!

109

GOOD-TO-THE-LAST-STITCH PINNING

Add one or more Good-to-the-Last-Stitch pins on the straight, open spaces between the points to accurately align the seam lines.

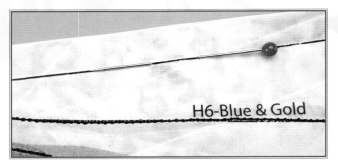

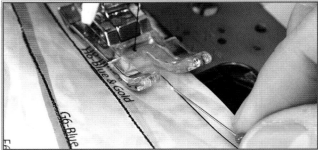

1 Place pins precisely along the seam lines on both the front and back. Stick them through at a very flat angle. (As with Acupoint pinning, don't stick-and-lean, as this will pull seam lines out of alignment.)

2 As you sew, leave the pin in until the point is ⅛" in front of the sewing machine needle. Grasp the head of the pin and continue to sew slowly, holding onto the pin head so that the fabric slides off the pin as it advances. This keeps the pinning absolutely secure and accurate until two stitches before passing under the needle, giving the layers no opportunity to slip out of alignment. This is particularly useful when sewing bulky areas together.

Bulky Seams

There's really no way to avoid bulky seams in spirals—they are a natural product of piling up layers of fabric at the corners of the triangles. If you used Nesting spirals or hybrid spirals and reduced seams where possible, you have at least minimized bulk where you could. One way to ease the bulk is to let seam allowances fall where they want to when pressing: Bulky areas will lie naturally over less bulky areas. If a seam allowance needs to change direction, that's okay. Press flat from the back, then gently flatten and press the seam from the front so that there is no twist or tuck. Don't clip the seam allowance.

Even if you are leaving in the foundation, remove the foundation from corners and other bulky areas as soon as you don't need the markings any more

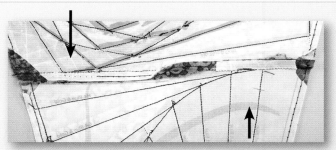

Same-direction spirals naturally place the bulkiest part of one spiral against the least bulky point of the adjoining spiral, so bulk is minimized.

(usually after sewing the first seam over the corner). Mark the intersection of the next seam at that corner to help you match points accurately. If you were going to remove the foundation anyway, it's a lot easier to remove it before it gets stitched into another seam.

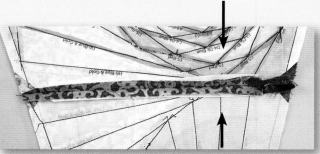

In adjoining opposite-direction spirals, the bulkiest parts of both spirals lie next to each other. There is no way to avoid this, but a few taps with a hammer help to flatten the bulk. Press the seam with steam first, so you can move your fingers out of the way. Then, give the seam a couple of medium-gentle taps from the back side. Do it on a rough or fabric-covered surface to prevent creating a shiny spot on the front.

JOINING SPIRALS AND WEDGES

To assemble your mandala, join the spirals together to form the wedges and the wedges together to form the mandala. If you are using a pieced background, add the background at this point as well.

1 First, place all of the spirals in their correct positions. If you are using a pieced background, position the background pieces as well. Pay attention to any variations in detail or fussy cutting to make sure these are positioned correctly.

2 Join all the spirals in each wedge and attach the corresponding background piece.

3 For 8-, 12- or 16-wedge mandalas, join wedges into quarters. In mandalas with mirror symmetry, join mirrored pairs of wedges.

4 Next, join the wedges or quarters into halves of the mandala. Join the halves together to complete the mandala. Stitch each seam in two parts, each starting from the center and going out to the edge.

TIP

In an 8- or 16-wedge mandala, join the wedges into triangle quarters, then add border strips before joining the quarters. This automatically miters the corners.

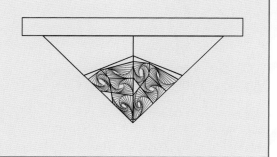

Successful Centers

As you sew wedges together, pay attention to the direction of seams at the center. Distribute the bulk as much as possible to help the center point match and lie flat. Plan ahead to avoid bulk at the center of your spira. See page 83 for ways to reduce the number of center seams.

"Pinwheel" pressing is one way you can arrange seams at the center: As you join wedges together, press all the seams in the same direction, either left or right.
The seams then lay flat around the center point, and the bulk is distributed evenly. This works particularly well in a mandala with rotational symmetry.

In mandalas with mirror symmetry, seams will naturally fall in mirrored symmetry, so let them. You'll also be able to press some seams open.

If you're not sure which way seams will fall best, stitch only to the intersection point of the seam line and then backstitch; don't cross any seam allowances. This will allow you to press the seam allowance in either direction, or to press it open, letting you distribute the bulk as you wish.

What if the wedges don't fit?

An ounce of prevention is worth a pound of cure, as they say, and if you tested the fit of the templates previously, they are virtually certain to fit together properly. However, if for some mysterious reason they don't at this point, here's what to do.

- First, press the mandala thoroughly. It's possible that any slack will smooth out when you do.
- Next, lay the mandala face down on a hard, flat surface. Get the mandala as flat and smooth as possible. Locate a seam where there is some slack—preferably where two wedges are in mirror symmetry. Take a tiny pinch in the seam to take up some of the slack in the mandala. Go to the other repetitions of that seam and take tiny pinches of slack in them as well. Take up all the slack in tiny adjustments spread evenly around the entire mandala.
- You might want to wait to make adjustments until the foundation is removed. Fabric does ease and stretch, and it might turn out that once the foundation is gone and the mandala is pressed well, the fabric will relax into a proper fit, or it can be eased into a fit without having to adjust seams.

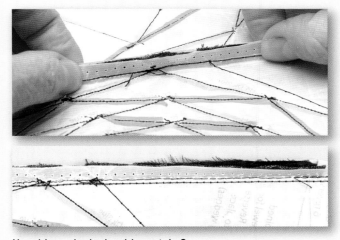

How big a pinch should you take?

When you pinch the seam, you take out double that width, because it comes from both sides of the seam. For example, if you take $\frac{1}{16}$" pinch, you take out $\frac{1}{8}$" of slack. Now, multiply that pinch by the number of seams that you adjust. For example, if you pinch 4 seams, that $\frac{1}{8}$" pinch gets multiplied by 4, for a total of $\frac{1}{2}$". So, take really small pinches, usually no more than $\frac{1}{16}$"—a tiny pinch in 3 or 4 seams will likely be enough to fix the problem.

SETTING A MANDALA ON A WHOLE-CLOTH BACKGROUND

If your mandala has a whole-cloth background rather than a pieced background, you will only need to assemble the mandala—there are no background pieces to add to the wedges. Once the mandala is assembled, sew a facing to the back of the mandala in order to turn the edge and appliqué the mandala to the background.

1 The facing fabric should be a square or rectangle at least as wide as the mandala. The color should match either the outside edge of the mandala or the background.

Press the mandala well with the foundation still in. Lay the facing fabric face up on your work surface. Pull it taut (but not tight) and tape it evenly around all sides. Lay the assembled mandala face down on the facing fabric.

2 Pin generously around the edge of the mandala. Before stitching around the mandala, remove the foundation from seam intersections (see page 110). Stitch along the seam lines at the edge of the foundation all the way around the mandala. Double-stitch over points or curves where you'll trim or clip the seam to turn it.

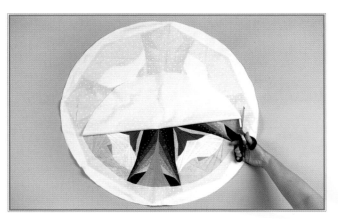

3 Cut away the center of the facing fabric, leaving 2"–3" inside the outer edge of the mandala. Clip the seam allowance where necessary to turn the seam smoothly, but don't clip unless it is necessary.

4 Remove the foundation around the outer edge seam of the mandala now, even if you plan to leave the rest of the foundation in. If you plan to remove all the foundation, do it now.

Turn the mandala right side out with the facing to the back. If there are points along the edge, place the tip of a pencil or a bamboo skewer in the point before turning it to keep the point sharp.

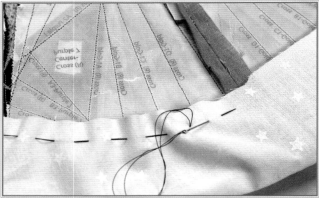

5 If the facing is a bit loose, stitch a running stitch around the edge of the facing and use it like a drawstring to tighten the facing.

6 Press the seam around the edge of the mandala so the facing doesn't show from the front. Bulky seams may not turn under enough to completely hide the edge of the facing—this is why you chose a matching fabric.

Once the edge is turned under, baste the mandala into position on the background. Appliqué the mandala to the background by hand or by machine with a narrow zigzag stitch that just catches the edge of the mandala.

When you are ready to quilt, if you want to reduce bulk, you can cut away the background fabric behind the mandala and also trim away excess facing fabric.

BORDERS

If necessary, square up the edges of the background, then attach the borders.

TIP

Instead of a facing, sew piping around the edge of the mandala. Turn it, then stitch-in-the-ditch between the mandala and the piping to attach the mandala to the background.

Finishing Your Spiral Mandala Quilt

Quilting your mandala adds another layer of artistry to the design. Here are techniques and ideas to guide and inspire you.

REMOVING FOUNDATIONS

If you used a removable foundation, wait to tear it out until after you have sewn the entire mandala together (except at bulky corners, as noted on page 110). Paper foundations should always be removed unless you want the added stiffness of the foundation and the quilt will never be washed. The best tool I have found for removing foundations is a bamboo skewer—it is sharp enough to score paper and fit into tight corners, but not sharp enough to tear fabric (thanks to Betsy Vinegrad, who taught me this). I also find tweezers useful. Remove as much paper as possible from narrow tips, since this is where the bulk is thickest already.

With nonwoven, tear-away foundation, you have the option to leave it in or remove it. Even if it starts out somewhat stiff, it will soften up with use over time.

QUILTING

As you realize by now, the piecing in a mandala is quite dense. Quilting by machine, rather than by hand, is the more practical choice. Use a strong, good-quality thread to minimize breakage and keep extra needles on hand in case you break one (or more). Plan your quilting to avoid extremely thick areas whenever possible.

Flow forms are usually the strongest design element in a spiral mandala, so let them guide you. Here are some suggestions to get you thinking—not necessarily to be used all at once!

- Follow the curves and shapes of the flow forms and spokes.
- Stitch-in-the-ditch along edges of spokes and flow forms.
- Follow the shape of the triangles that form flow forms and spokes.
- Contain different textures within adjacent flow forms.
- Use the same quilting pattern over areas you want to relate or unify.
- Quilt lightly or not at all over some areas such as thin spokes, then quilt heavily around them to make them stand out.
- Echo the spiral theme in non-spiral areas of your quilt.
- Draw out motifs from the fabrics for quilting design.

Backgrounds present their own opportunities and challenges. Use the corners around a mandala to incorporate design elements that emphasize the design (and even the message) of the mandala, rather than simply filling in space with texture. If you use templates, they will probably require some adjustment to fit around the curved edge of a mandala.

BINDING

Measure all the way around your finished quilt and cut enough strips 2½" wide to equal that measurement plus 2½" per strip to allow for bias seams joining the strips. Add 8"–10" for mitered corners. If you are binding only straight edges, binding strips can be cut on-grain. If you are binding curved edges, binding strips must be cut on the bias.

Complete instructions for applying a standard double-fold binding are on the CD included with this book. They can also be found at http://spiromaniacs.files.wordpress.com/2008/09/binding-a-quilt.pdf. If you need in-person help, an experienced quilter at your local quilt shop or guild can help. Many professional machine quilters offer binding service as well.

Congratulations—you have finished a beautiful spiral mandala quilt!

CHAPTER THREE

Projects

I hope by now you're feeling excited and inspired to make a spiral mandala quilt!

In the introduction I said that this book was designed to be used in three ways: to make a project from the book, to create your own design using the templates provided or to create your own design from scratch.

This chapter contains six spiral mandala quilt patterns that are ready to make. If you prefer the first approach, you can make any of these quilts just as they are shown.

If you prefer to design your own spiral mandala quilt but want a jump-start, you can begin with the templates for these patterns and create your own interpretation of the design. There are also additional wedge puzzles on the accompanying CD that can be used in the same way.

If you prefer to make your own spiral mandala quilt from scratch, you can still use the patterns here by studying them to see the techniques used.

I've designed these spiral mandala quilts to include and demonstrate as many of the concepts in this book as I could. The patterns are presented from simplest to most complex. With each pattern I've listed the type of wedge, type of symmetry and other techniques that are demonstrated in the pattern. I also discuss my fabric and design choices.

Whether you make a quilt from one of these patterns, or simply use them as learning tools and inspiration for your own design, I hope they will help you to develop a deeper understanding of spirals and quilt design in general, and in the process challenge and encourage your own creativity.

Instructions for All Projects

PATTERNS AND INSTRUCTIONS

Templates for all of the projects are on the CD in both .pdf and EQ format. The .pdf files can be opened with Adobe Acrobat. Most computers already have Acrobat installed. If yours does not, you can download Acrobat for free at www.adobe.com. EQ files can be opened in Electric Quilt version 6 or 7.

FOUNDATIONS

Make one copy of all foundations on white paper. Mark your personal changes in fabric/color placement, then make a copy of the marked foundation. Keep one copy for reference, the other copy is used for cutting templates (see page 94).

Make or print enough copies of all foundations on translucent foundation material so that you have one foundation for each spiral in the mandala. Assemble any foundations that print in sections. Lay out all foundations and mark which ones are reverse according to instructions on page 95.

Print one copy of the background templates (if used) on white paper.

Test all foundations and templates for fit (see page 87) before beginning to sew, as photocopiers and printers often have a bit of distortion.

TEMPLATE NUMBERING

All the spirals have the same position numbers on their pieces (A1, A2, etc.), so it is important to know which piece goes in which spiral. Each spiral is named or numbered; the name or number of the spiral is on each piece in that spiral. To avoid confusion, you might find it helpful to cut and sew all copies of only one spiral at the same time.

FABRIC YARDAGE

The yardage tables in this book and on the CD give the minimum yardage needed to make each quilt using the cutting instructions on pages 97–99. This measurement is based on three factors: 1) fabric that is 44" wide, 2) the amount of fabric is rounded up to the nearest 1/8 yard and 3) rectangular strips of fabric are cut no more than 1/4" larger on each side of their templates. (I have given the yardage this way so that if you are working with fabric you already have, rather than buying fabric, you will know if it is really enough.) If your fabric is less than 44" wide, if you cut the strips of fabric more generously or if you want "insurance," you will want more yardage than what is shown in the table.

When buying fussy cuts, buy the number of motifs that you need. If cutting one motif with a seam

allowance means cutting into another repeat of that motif, you'll need to buy twice as many motifs.

In addition to the yardage table in the book, the CD contains a more comprehensive yardage chart that includes fabric swatches. You can compare your fabric choices with the swatches in the table by placing your swatches alongside the ones shown, but keep in mind that monitor and printer settings are different on each machine, so your printouts may not be color correct. Making black and white photocopies of both the swatches from the book and your own swatches will help you compare value.

Each mandala can be colored in many ways. A line drawing of each project mandala is included on the CD so you can easily experiment with your own coloring. Changing the coloring will change the yardage required.

CUTTING FABRICS

Refer to cutting instructions on pages 97–99. Lay out the cutting templates on the whole fabric as shown, grouping templates of the same or similar height in the same row. (This conserves fabric.) Cut width of fabric (WOF) strips 1/4" higher than the templates. Cutting this way will give you the number of strips shown in the cutting table. (The number of strips in the tables is a guideline and your number of strips may vary slightly depending on how you lay out the cutting templates.) Do not cut the strips in the cutting table and then try to fit the templates on the strips.

After cutting strips, cut them down to rectangles for each spiral piece that are 1/4" larger than the template on each side. Clip together all the pieces for each ring and group them in order (Ring A, Ring B, etc.) by spiral. Cut borders and any pieces that have an exact shape according to instructions in the cutting list and on the template.

SEWING THE SPIRALS AND ASSEMBLING THE MANDALA

Each spiral is labeled with its type. Follow the instructions on pages 104–105 for sewing Nesting and Baravelle spirals, or on pages 106–108 for Pinwheel and Point-to-Point spirals. If there are any exceptions or special instructions for sewing a particular spiral, those instructions are printed on the foundation to which they apply.

Assemble the mandala according to the instructions on pages 109–115. Any instructions that differ from the standard methods are given in the instructions for that project.

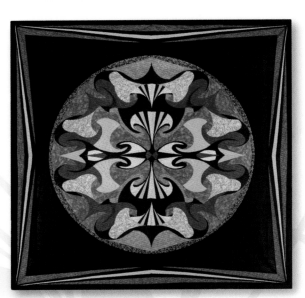

CREST OF THE CRANE

Finished size: 33" × 33"; Mandala size: 10⅜" radius (20¾" diameter)

Two fabrics containing cranes in different sizes inspired this Asian-themed mandala.

This quilt is the result of the Blind Man's Bluff and wedge puzzle techniques found on pages 10–11. It uses an asymmetrical wedge set in mirror symmetry. The size of the cranes determined the overall size of the mandala; if you use appliqué in a similar way, size the mandala so that it is proportional to the fussy-cut motifs. You can also make the mandala without the appliqué elements.

What you'll learn in this mandala: Nesting spirals, mirror symmetry, double-wide method for reducing center seams, value gradation, energy and jewelry fabrics, appliqué background, pre-quilting appliqué motifs

120

COLOR (POSITION)	FABRIC TYPE	MIN. AMOUNT	CUTTING INSTRUCTIONS (READ PAGES 96–99 AND 118 BEFORE CUTTING)
Large Cranes (Appliqué)	Jewelry	Enough to fussy cut desired motif(s)	Pre-quilt appliqué motif(s) (see Quilting, page 123), then cut out motif(s) leaving ¼" seam allowance on all sides.
Small Cranes (Background)	Jewelry	⅞ yd	29" square
Green 1 (Spirals)	Foundation	⅛ yd	2 strips 1" × WOF
Green 2 (Spirals)	Energy	⅛ yd	2 strips 1" × WOF
Green 3 (Spirals)	Energy	⅛ yd	2 strips 1" × WOF
Green 4 (Spirals)	Energy or Foundation	⅛ yd	2 strips 1" × WOF
Pink 1 (Spirals)	Foundation	⅛ yd	4 strips 1" × WOF
Pink 2 (Spirals)	Foundation	⅛ yd	2 strips 1" × WOF
Pink 3 (Spirals)	Foundation	⅛ yd	2 strips 1" × WOF
Pink 4 (Spirals)	Energy or Foundation	⅛ yd	2 strips 1" × WOF
Blue 1 (Spirals)	Foundation	⅛ yd	2 strips 1" × WOF
Blue 2 (Spirals)	Energy or Foundation	⅛ yd	4 strips 1" × WOF
Blue 3 (Spirals)	Energy or Foundation	¼ yd	5 strips 1" × WOF
Blue 4 (Spirals, Facing, Border 2, Binding)	Foundation	1⅜ yds	7 strips 1" × WOF 21" square (facing) 4 strips 2" × WOF (Border 2) 4 strips 2½" × WOF (Binding)
Gold 1 (Spirals, Center)	Jewelry	⅛ yd (or enough to cut WOF strips + 5 fussy-cut motifs for Piece #D2)	2 strips 1" × WOF 1 strip 1¾" × WOF or 5 fussy cuts (Point spiral Piece #D2)
Gold 2 (Spirals)	Foundation	⅛ yd	2 strips 1" × WOF
Sparkle (Spirals, Border 1)	Foundation	¼ yd	2 strips 1" × WOF 3 strips 1¼" × WOF 4 strips 1" × WOF (Border)
White (Spirals)	Foundation	⅜ yd	8 strips 1" × WOF
Backing and Hanging Sleeve	Any	1½ yds	41" square for Backing 9" × WOF strip for Hanging Sleeve
Lightweight Muslin or White Fabric	Enough to back fussy-cut motifs from Large Crane/appliqué fabric		
Batting	1 yd (at least 34" × 34" square), plus enough to back appliqué motifs		
Translucent Foundation Sheets	15 sheets 8½" × 11"		
White paper	12 sheets 8½" × 11"		

Templates and a fabric selection guide are on the CD accompanying this book. Read pages 96–97 before buying fabric. Follow the instructions found previously in this book to sew spirals and assemble the mandala. Instructions particular to this quilt are given on pages 122–123.

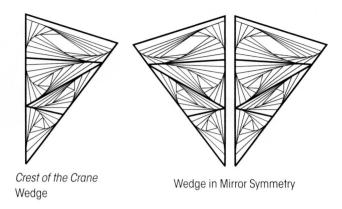

Crest of the Crane
Wedge

Wedge in Mirror Symmetry

SEWING THE SPIRALS

All spirals in this mandala are Nesting spirals. There are 5 "Right" and 5 "Left" of each spiral. See the notes on all of the templates on the CD regarding the center pieces combined with triangles in the first ring. Also see the note on the Point spiral template regarding combined Piece #D2. (See page 83 fo more helpful information about this.) Because pieces are narrow, use an Add-an-Eighth tool when doing the next step trims. After sewing spirals, trim ¼" outside all straight edges of each spiral for a seam allowance.

PREPARING FOUNDATIONS AND CUTTING TEMPLATES

One wedge makes up this mandala; it is repeated 10 times in 5 mirrored pairs. Templates are provided in both original and reverse orientation (denoted as Right and Left on templates). There is no need to make two sets of cutting templates because all of the fabric is cut in rectangular strips, not triangles; each strip of fabric will work in either original or reverse orientation.

ASSEMBLING THE WEDGES AND MANDALA

After sewing the individual spirals, join the spirals into wedges to make 5 "Left" wedges and 5 "Right" wedges. Even if you plan to leave in the foundation, remove as much as possible where seams intersect, to reduce bulk after sewing one seam over the corner (see page 110).

1. Join Middle A and Middle B; attach Point and Outer spirals to top and bottom of the Middles.

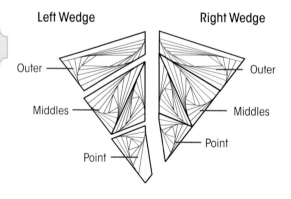

Left Wedge   Right Wedge

Outer   Outer

Middles   Middles

Point   Point

2. Join five pairs of Left-Right wedges along the seam line of piece D2 in the Point spiral. To begin, sew precisely to the upper point of the double-wide piece and backstitch.

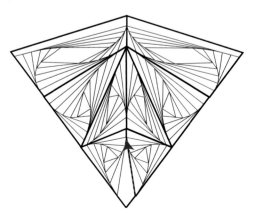

CUTTING FABRIC

Cut fabric according to the instructions outlined on pages 96–99 and 118.

3. Pin the remainder of the seam between the two wedges, aligning all matching points. Sew, beginning at point of Piece #D2 (backstitch just to point); continue stitching toward the outside edge of the wedge.

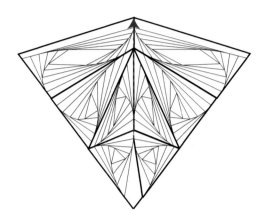

4. Join wedges: Sew one group of two wedge pairs and one group of three wedge pairs. Carefully match the seam lines and points where the triangles meet (see Pinning Techniques, page 109–110).

Join the two groups of wedges. Sew two seams, each from center to edge. Avoid stitching over previously sewn seams at the center point, so that the bulk of the seam allowance can be distributed evenly after sewing.

Press well, letting bulky seams fall in their natural direction.

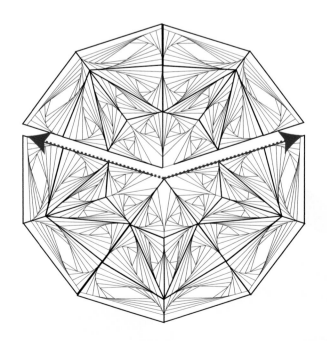

5. Sew a facing to the mandala following the instructions on pages 113–114. Appliqué the mandala to the Background square. Square up the Background if necessary.
6. Sew Border 1 to the sides of the Background square. Trim the ends even with the edges of the Background. Sew Border 1 to the top and bottom of the Background square. Trim the ends even with the edges of the previously sewn Border 1 strips.
7. Sew Border 2 to the sides of the Background square. Trim the ends even with the edges of the Background. Sew Border 2 to the top and bottom of the Background square. Trim the ends even with the edges of the previously sewn Border 2 strips.

If you are removing the foundation, remove it all now. If you are leaving the foundation in and you used tape to hold the center piece of fabric, tear out the foundation at the center of each spiral and remove the tape.

QUILTING

Quilt the mandala as desired. After quilting, square up if necessary.
QUILTING FUSSY-CUT MOTIFS
Layer the fussy-cut motif, batting and lightweight muslin. Quilt as desired, then trim the motif to ¼" outside the edges of the design.

BINDING

This quilt uses a standard folded binding ½" wide. Join the binding strips with diagonal seams at the ends, then press in half lengthwise. Set the raw edges of the binding at the trimmed edge of the quilt and stitch a generous ¼" inside the raw edges of the binding. Turn the folded edge to the back and hand-stitch it in place to finish. Complete illustrated instructions can be found on the CD that came with this book.

APPLIQUÉ

Position the appliqué motifs over the surface of the quilted mandala. Hand-appliqué them into position, passing the needle between the layers of the quilted mandala so the stitches do not show on the back of the quilt. Tuck small pieces of batting between the appliqué and the surface of the quilt if you want more height in the appliqué. Remove batting from narrow areas such as the beak and legs.

FINISH

Add a label and hanging sleeve, if desired.

EASTER MANDALA

Finished size: 35½" × 35½"; Mandala size: 15" radius (30" diameter)

Two symbols of Easter—lilies and a Celtic cross—combine to create this mandala made in purple and gold, the liturgical colors of the Easter season.

This mandala combines two different wedges. The Cross wedge contains two identical spirals in mirrored symmetry. The Lily/Leaf wedge is a Type 2 symmetrical wedge (see page 35); the leaf spirals are in mirrored symmetry and the lily spiral spins in a single direction. The Cross wedge is combined with the Lily/Leaf wedge to make one quarter of the mandala. This quarter-circle repeats around the mandala in compound rotational symmetry.

What you'll learn in this mandala: Nesting and Pinwheel spirals, Type 2 symmetrical wedge, pieced spiral center, compound rotational symmetry, steering a Pinwheel spiral, wrap-over and cut-off methods of reducing center seams, T-joints, value gradation, appliqué background

COLOR (POSITION)	FABRIC TYPE	MIN. AMOUNT	CUTTING INSTRUCTIONS (READ PAGES 96–99 AND 118 BEFORE CUTTING)
Gold (Cross, Gold Mandala Border, Center of Lily, Binding)	Foundation	⅞ yd	4 strips 1" × WOF 4 strips 1⅛" × WOF 2 strips 1¼" × WOF 4 strips 1⅜" × WOF 4 strips 3½" × WOF for ¾" binding
Light Blue (Background behind Lily)	Foundation	⅜ yd	2 strips 1" × WOF 1 strip 1¼" × WOF 2 strips 1½" × WOF 2 strips 1¾" × WOF 1 strip 3¼" × WOF
White (Lily, White Mandala Border, Square Border 2, Facing)	Foundation	1½ yds	(See cutting diagram on CD) 1 strip 1" × WOF 1 strip 1⅛" × WOF 2 strips 1¼" × WOF 1 strip 1¾" × WOF 4 strips 2" × WOF 31" square (or larger) for facing 4 strips 1½" × 36" for Border
Green (Leaves)	Foundation	⅛ yd	4 strips 1⅛" × WOF
Magenta (Square Border 1)	Foundation	¼ yd	4 strips 1¾" × WOF
Seven shades of purple in gradation from light to dark:			
Purple 1 (Lightest)	Foundation	⅛ yd	1 strip 1¾" × WOF
Purple 2	Foundation	⅛ yd	2 strips 1½" × WOF
Purple 3	Foundation	⅛ yd	2 strips 1½" × WOF
Purple 4	Foundation	⅛ yd	2 strips 1½" × WOF
Purple 5	Energy or Foundation	¼ yd	3 strips 1⅝" × WOF
Purple 6	Foundation	¼ yd	2 strips 1⅛" × WOF 2 strips 1½" × WOF
Purple 7 (Darkest)	Foundation	1⅛ yds	(See cutting diagram on CD) 2 strips 1" × LOF 4 strips 1¼" × LOF 2 strips 1¾" × LOF 33" square for Background (If desired, cut larger and trim to size after appliquéing mandala to background.)
Backing and Hanging Sleeve	Any	1½ yds	44" square for Backing 9" × 36" strip for Hanging Sleeve
Batting	1 yd (at least 36" × 36" square)		
Translucent Foundation Sheets	20 sheets 8½" × 11"		
White paper	10 sheets 8½" × 11"		

Templates and a fabric selection guide are on the CD accompanying this book. Read pages 96–97 before buying fabric. Follow the instructions found previously in this book to sew spirals and assemble the mandala. Instructions particular to this quilt are given on pages 126–127.

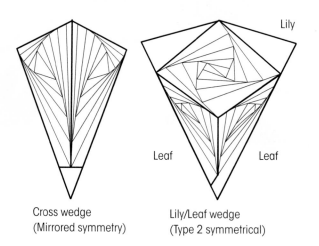

Cross wedge
(Mirrored symmetry)

Lily/Leaf wedge
(Type 2 symmetrical)

PREPARING FOUNDATIONS AND CUTTING TEMPLATES

There are two different wedges in this mandala—the Lily/Leaf and the Cross. The Cross wedge is joined to the left side of the Lily/Leaf wedge to make four quarter-circles.

Leaf spirals and Cross spirals: There are 8 total of each of these spirals; 4 of each are in original orientation and 4 of each are in reverse (mirror) orientation. Templates are provided in both original and reverse orientation. There is no need to make two sets of cutting templates because all fabric is cut as rectangular strips, not triangles; each strip of fabric will work in either original or reverse orientation.

Lily spirals: There are 4 of these spirals, all in the same orientation.

Printing Templates

Print on white paper: 2 each of Lily, Leaf and Cross spiral foundations (keep one set of spirals as master templates and use the other set for cutting templates). Assemble Cross and Lily, Parts 1 and 2. Cut Gold and White border pieces off Cross and Lily and join them along dashed line for border templates.

Print on translucent foundation paper: 4 each of Lily, Leaf and Cross spiral foundations. Assemble Cross and Lily, Parts 1 and 2. Do not cut off Gold and White border pieces from foundations.

To print templates from EQ: In addition to the PDF version of this pattern, templates are also provided in EQ6. Before using the EQ file to make this quilt, read the file on this CD entitled "Using EQ Project Files." This contains important information that will impact the successful outcome of your project.

CUTTING FABRIC

Cut fabric according to the instructions outlined on pages 96–99 and 118, using the cutting templates on white paper.

SEWING THE SPIRALS

The Cross and Leaf spirals are Nesting spirals. The Lily is a Pinwheel spiral. Special instructions regarding the centers and tips of the spirals are given on the templates (see page 83). Read and follow these instructions carefully. After sewing the spirals, trim ¼" outside all straight edges of each spiral for seam allowances.

ASSEMBLING THE WEDGES AND MANDALA

After sewing all individual spirals, assemble the quarter-circle wedges in this order. Even if you plan to leave in foundation, remove foundation at corners where seams intersect to reduce bulk after sewing one seam over the corner (see page 110).

1. Join the Leaf spirals along the center seam. Sew D3(R) over D3; this is a "Y" seam (see page 109).

2. Join the Lily spirals to the Leaf spirals (this is also a "Y" seam).

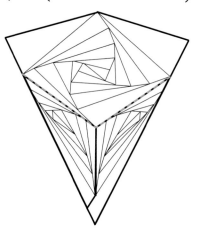

3. Join the Cross spirals in pairs. Sew the Shared Tip across the bottom of the pair. (This eliminates one center seam.) Trim the tip to the shape of the foundation plus a ¼" seam allowance.

Join each Cross assembly to the left side of a Lily/Leaf assembly to make the four quarters of the mandala.

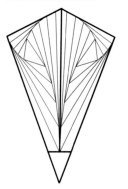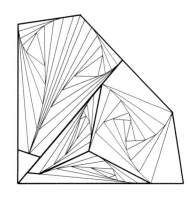

4. Join the four quarters to make the full mandala.

5. Sew the Gold Border pieces in counterclockwise order around edges of mandala. Leave a partially unsewn end on the first piece so you can sew it over the last piece. Each piece overlaps the piece sewn before it around the circle. Complete the partial seam of the first piece over the last. Do a next step trim.

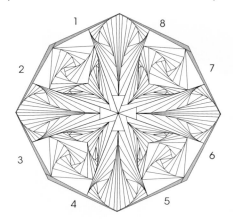

6. Repeat Step 6 for White Border pieces. Do not trim the outside edge after sewing the White Border.

7. Sew a facing to the mandala following the instructions on pages 113–114. Appliqué the mandala to the Background square. Square up the background if necessary.

8. Sew Square Border 1 (Magenta) to the sides of the Background square. Trim the ends even with the edges of the Background. Sew Square Border 1 to the top and bottom of the Background square. Trim the ends even with the edges of the previous Border 1 strips.

9. Sew Square Border 2 (White) to the sides of the Background square. Trim the ends even with the edges of the Background. Sew Square Border 2 to the top and bottom of the Background square. Trim the ends even with the edges of the previous Border 2 strips.

If you are removing the foundation, remove it all now. If you are leaving the foundation in, and you used tape to hold the center piece of fabric, tear out the foundation at the center of each spiral and remove the tape.

QUILT

Quilt as desired. Square up after quilting if necessary.

BINDING

This quilt uses a standard folded binding, but it is ¾" wide instead of ½" wide. After quilting, square up the quilt to ½" outside the edges of Border 2. Set the raw edges of the binding ½" from the edge of the quilt (even with the edge of Border 2) and stitch ¼" inside the raw edges of the binding. This leaves ¾" between the binding seam and the edge of the quilt. Complete illustrated instructions for binding can be found on the CD that came with this book.

FINISH

Add a label and hanging sleeve, if desired.

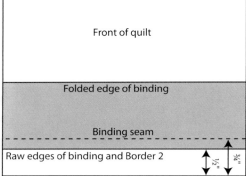

Raw edges of batting and backing

ELIZABETH

Finished size: 58" × 58"; Mandala size: 20" radius (40" diameter)

Rich reds, royal blues, elegant fabrics and lots of shimmering gold give the royal treatment to this quilt inspired by a queen.

Two spiral direction variations and three different colorations of the same wedge give this design both unity and variety. An energy fabric (gold and blue) fills the background negative space, allowing blue and red foundation fabrics to stand out over it. Jewelry fabrics fill the centers of the spirals, and a strong border print creates a regal frame.

What you'll learn in this mandala: Nesting and hybrid spirals, spiral direction, compound mirror symmetry, appliqué center method of reducing center seams, pieced background

COLOR (POSITION)	FABRIC TYPE	MIN. AMOUNT	CUTTING INSTRUCTIONS (READ PAGES 96–99 AND 118 BEFORE CUTTING)
Dark Blue (Spirals, Background)	Foundation	1¾ yds	1 strip ¾" × WOF (Point spiral H2) 2 strips 1" × WOF (Point spirals) 7 strips 1⅛" × WOF (Outer spirals A, B, C, D, E, F and H) 5 strips 1¼" × WOF (Outer spiral G; Point spirals) 1 strip 1½" × WOF (Point spirals) 16 pieces 4½" × 3" (Outer spirals, corner jewels) or 24, if no fussy-cut jewels 4 Corner Background 4 Side Background 4 Side Background reversed
Medium Blue (Spirals)	Foundation	1 yd	6 strips 1" × WOF (Point spirals F1, G1, H1) 15 strips 1¼" × WOF (Point spirals D1, E1, E3, F3, G3; Outer spirals A, B, C, D, E, F and H) 5 strips 1⅜" × WOF (Outer spiral G; Point spirals D3, H3)
Blue and Gold (Spirals)	Energy	⅞ yd	1 strip 1⅛" × WOF (Outer spirals A6, B6) 4 strips 1¼" × WOF (Point spirals A4, B4, C4, D4) 6 strips 1⅜" × WOF (Point spirals E4, F4, G4, H4) 6 strips 1½" × WOF (Outer spirals C6, F6, G6, H6) 2 strips 1¾" × WOF (Outer spirals D6, E6)
Red (Spirals)	Foundation	⅝ yd	7 strips 1" × WOF (Outer spirals A1, B1, H1, A5, B5, E5 and F5) 5 strips 1¼" × WOF (Outer spirals, all other templates) 4 strips 1⅜" × WOF (Point spirals, all templates except C3) 1 strip 1⅝" × WOF (Point spiral C3)
Gold 1 (Spirals)	Foundation	½ yd	3 strips ¾" × WOF (Point spirals D2, E2, F2, G2) 8 strips 1" × WOF (Outer spirals A, B, C, D and E; Point spirals A2, B2, C2) 5 strips 1¼" × WOF (Outer spirals F, G and H)
Gold 2 (Edge of Mandala, Inner Border)	Foundation	½ yd (or enough to fussy-cut)	6 strips 1¼" × WOF then joined into 4 strips 60" long (piece as necessary) (Inner border) 4 strips 1½" × WOF, then cut down to three 12" strips (Edge around mandala) Note: This striped fabric was fussy-cut along the LOF for the original quilt
Jewels (Centers of Spirals, Center of Mandala)	Jewelry	29 jewels approximately 3" in diameter, plus seam allowance (take the template to the store to check size)	Quantity of fabric will depend on number of motifs in fabric. (See info about buying fussy cuts on page 97.) 12 for Outer spirals 12 for Point spirals 4 for Edge (Jewels may be cut as 1-Piece Corner Jewels or 2-Piece Corner Jewels.) 1 for Center

COLOR (POSITION)	FABRIC TYPE	MIN. AMOUNT	CUTTING INSTRUCTIONS (READ PAGES 96-99 AND 118 BEFORE CUTTING)
Border print (Spirals, Outer Border)	Jewelry	1¾ yds if border pattern is repeated 4 times across WOF. May be more depending on size and repetition of pattern.	4 strips 60" long. (Outer border) Note: 60" strip length is long enough to miter corners. Width of strips depends on width of pattern in border print—the border shown here was cut 6½" wide. You may need additional fabric if the border pattern is printed less than 4 times across WOF, to center symmetrical prints and/or to match mitered corners.
Binding	Foundation	½ yd	6 strips 2½" × WOF. Join diagonally at ends for one continuous strip 240" total length
Backing and Hanging Sleeve	Any	3¾ yds	Cut 2 66" lengths of fabric and sew together along selvages. Trim to 66" square. Use trimmed fabric for hanging sleeve. To use less fabric for backing, include some fabric in backing left over from fussy cutting border print, if any.
Batting	60" square		
Translucent Foundation Sheets	36 sheets 8½" × 11"		
White paper	20 sheets 8½" × 11"		

Templates and a fabric selection guide are on the CD accompanying this book. Read pages 96–97 before buying fabric. Follow the instructions found previously in this book to sew spirals and assemble the mandala. Instructions particular to this quilt are given on pages 130–133.

PREPARING FOUNDATIONS AND CUTTING TEMPLATES

This mandala uses a single symmetrical wedge skeleton that contains only two spirals. The wedge has two variations, created by changing the spiral directions within it. When both spirals spin in the same direction, you get the trunk wedge; when the spirals spin in opposite directions, you get the fan wedge.

Each quarter of the mandala contains two trunk wedges and one fan wedge. Each of these three wedges is colored differently. The quarter-circle is repeated in compound mirrored symmetry across the vertical and horizontal axes.

Outer spiral: There are 12 total of these, 6 original and 6 reverse. They are all colored the same.

Point spirals #1, #2 and #3: There are 2 original and 2 reverse of each. Point #1 has the red fabric, Points #2 and #3 have slight differences in the placement of dark blue and gold. Watch the templates carefully.

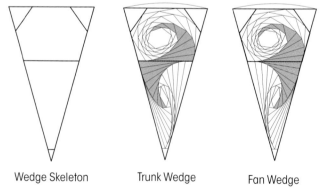

Wedge Skeleton   Trunk Wedge   Fan Wedge

Printing Templates

Print on white paper:
2 each Outer spiral, Point Spiral #1, Point Spiral #2 and Point Spiral #3. (Keep one set of spirals as master templates and use the other set for cutting templates). Assemble Point spirals (Parts 1 and 2).
1 Background Side, assemble Parts 1 and 2
1 Background Corner, assemble Parts 1, 2, 3 and 4

Print on translucent foundation paper:
12 Outer spiral, turn over 6 and mark R—this is now the front of these foundations
4 Point Spiral #1, turn over 2 and mark R—this is now the front of these foundations
4 Point Spiral #2, turn over 2 and mark R—this is now the front of these foundations
4 Point Spiral #3, turn over 2 and mark R—this is now the front of these foundations

To Print Templates from EQ: In addition to the PDF version of this pattern, templates are also provided in EQ6. Before using the EQ file to make this quilt, read the file on the CD entitled "Using EQ Project Files." This contains important information that will impact the successful outcome of your project.

CUTTING FABRIC

Cut fabric according to the instructions outlined on pages 96–99 and pages 118, using the cutting templates on white paper.

SEWING THE SPIRALS

It is very important to plan the placement of all fussy-cut elements before sewing any spirals.

The Point spirals are Nesting spirals. The Outer spirals begin with Nesting rings on the outside and work into a Baravelle spiral within. Sew both per instructions on pages 104–105 for Nesting and Baravelle spirals. When you reach the corner jewels of the Outer spirals, use the instructions for 2-Piece Corner Jewels on this page for solid blue jewels and the instructions for 1-Piece Corner Jewels on page 132 for single-piece fussy-cut jewels.

2-PIECE CORNER JEWELS

As you can see in the picture on page 128, if you look at the quilt as a clock face I used solid blue 2-Piece Corner Jewels at 1:00, 2:00, 4:00, 5:00, 7:00, 8:00, 10:00 and 11:00.

1. Trim the outer spiral seam allowance to ¼", then attach jewels to upper sides of spiral.

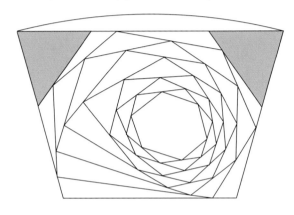

2. Sew the outer edge strip completely along the seam line.

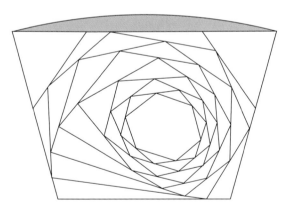

1-PIECE CORNER JEWELS

For corner jewels that are single pieces bridging two wedges, leave a window in the jewel space. I used 1Piece Corner Jewels in my quilt at 12:00, 3:00, 6:00 and 9:00. After joining the wedges, you'll reverse appliqué the jewel into the back of the window.

1. Trim ¼" beyond all outer edges of spirals for seam allowance, except do not trim the seam allowance along the edge where the window will be (arrow in diagram below). (This leaves a comfortable seam allowance to fold back for reverse appliqué.) Sew the solid blue corner into place.

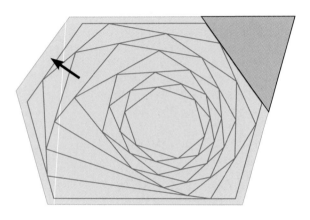

2. Sew the outer edge strip to the foundation as if the jewel fabric were in place, but do not sew the portion of the seam marked by a dashed red line between the red dots so you don't catch the open seam allowance in this seam. Where there is no fabric, sew the outer strip to the empty foundation paper.

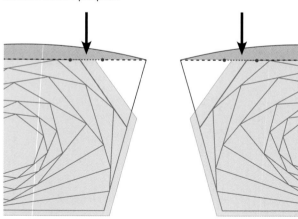

ASSEMBLING THE WEDGES AND MANDALA

(The techniques and photos on pages 109–112 show the assembly of the spirals and background this quilt. Instructions for inserting jewels in the windows follow here.)

Before sewing the spirals together, arrange the spirals, jewels and background pieces in their final positions. Look at the picture on page 128 for correct positioning.

Sew the background pieces to the corresponding outer spirals, using matching marks to align curved edges. On Outer spirals that have open windows, open the seam allowance of the outer strip to sew the fabric flat to the background. Even if you plan to leave in the foundation, remove foundation at corners where the seams intersect to reduce bulk after sewing one seam across the corner (see page 110).

Sew the Point spirals to their corresponding Outer spiral/Background assemblies to make 12 wedges (use the photo on page 128 as a placement guide).

Sew together each pair of wedges that has a corner jewel window between them. At the bottom of the window, stop the seam and backstitch. At the top of the window, sew the outer edge and background pieces together, carefully matching the folded bottom edge of the outer edge strip. Backstitch at the edge of the window (red dashed lines in the diagram below).

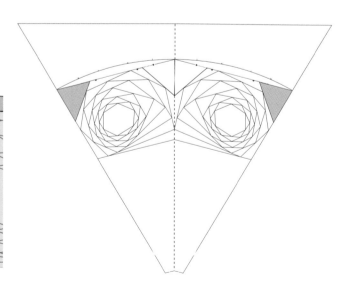

Remove the foundation paper in the window and fold the seam allowances in the window back over the edges of the spiral foundation. Press the folded edge and pin the seam allowance into place. Position the fussy-cut jewel behind the window. Baste and then reverse appliqué into place by hand or machine.

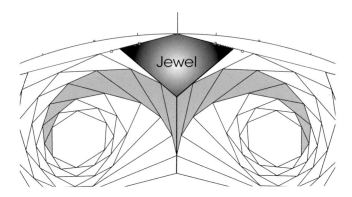

Join wedges into groups of 3 wedges (four quarters of the mandala), then join the quarters to make the full mandala.

Press well. Allow bulky seam allowances to fall where they naturally want to go, but press carefully on the front at these places to avoid twists or tucks in seams. Do not clip seam allowances.

APPLIQUÉ CENTER

After joining all wedges, appliqué the center jewel over the space at the center of the mandala.

To prepare a perfect circle, cut a circle of cardboard (such as a cereal box) in the size you want the circle to be. Cut a circle of fabric about ½" larger than the circle on all sides. Hand-sew a running stitch with strong thread all the way around the fabric about ¼" from the edge. Use a solid anchoring knot at the beginning and leave the end of the thread loose—don't knot the finishing end. Next, heat up your iron. Place the fabric face down on the ironing board and place the cardboard circle in the center of the fabric. Pull on the loose end of the thread to tighten the fabric around the circle. Press well while holding the thread tight.

Appliqué the circle to the center of the mandala over the open space. (You might find it helpful to leave the cardboard in until you're finished, then tear it out.)

BORDERS

Sew the Inner Border to the inside edges of the Outer Border. Sew the border units to all sides; end seam and backstitch exactly at the point where the corner seam allowances would intersect, so the seams are set up for mitering corners.

Miter the corners, matching the Inner Border/Outer Border seam. If the pattern of the fabric is symmetrical and will align at the corners, use pins to match the pattern as well (see Acupoint Pinning, page 109). Trim off any excess fabric inside the corner seam.

If you are removing the foundation, remove it all now. If you are leaving the foundation in, and you used tape to hold the centers of the spirals, tear out the foundation at the center of each spiral and remove the tape.

QUILTING

Quilt as desired. If necessary, square up after quilting.

BINDING

This quilt uses a standard folded binding ½" wide. Join the binding strips with diagonal seams at the ends, then press in half lengthwise. Set the raw edges of the binding at the trimmed edge of the quilt and stitch a generous ¼" inside the raw edges of the binding. Turn the folded edge to the back and hand-stitch in place to finish. Complete illustrated instructions can be found on the CD that came with this book.

FINISH

Add a label and hanging sleeve, if desired.

THAT'S THE WAY LOVE IS

Finished size: 49½" × 49½"; Mandala size: 16½" radius (33" diameter)
Quilted by Karen Overton

Butterflies in your stomach, stars in your eyes, a spinning, swirling dance in your step. . . that's the way love (or at least infatuation) is!

Fabric selection for this quilt is easy—choose a medium to large, multicolor print for the border, then pull solid colors from that fabric for the mandala. Select a background that lets the rest of the colors pop. Here, the colors, theme and even the quilting pattern come from the butterflies in the border. Parts of the mandala are "blacked out" by filling them with the background fabric. This gives the mandala its open, lacy feel and scalloped edge. This mandala uses an asymmetrical wedge with matching side nodes, set in rotational symmetry. It is the same wedge used in *Crimes of Passion* on page 138. What a difference a change in symmetry and color can make!

What you'll learn in this mandala: Nesting spirals, rotational symmetry, solid flow forms, negative space, scalloped edges, pieced background

COLOR (POSITION)	FABRIC TYPE	MIN. AMOUNT	CUTTING INSTRUCTIONS (READ PAGES 96–99 AND 118 BEFORE CUTTING)
Butterflies (Borders)	Jewelry	1½ yds if not pieced ¾ yd if pieced (See note in Backing fabric.)	4 strips 3¾" × 50" or 8 strips 3¾" × 25¼"
Pink (Spirals)	Foundation	½ yd	4 strips ¾" × WOF 12 strips 1" × WOF 1 strip 1½" × WOF
Blue (Spirals, Binding)	Foundation	⅝ yd	2 strips ¾" × WOF 4 strips ⅞" × WOF 5 strips 1" × WOF 1 strip 1⅛" × WOF 1 strip 1½" × WOF 5 strips 2½" × WOF (Binding)
Tan (Spirals)	Foundation	⅜ yd	6 strips 1" × WOF 4 strips 1⅛" × WOF
Black (Spirals)	Foundation	⅜ yd	2 strips ¾" × WOF 12 strips ⅞" × WOF
Cream (Spirals, Background)	Foundation	2½ yds	4 strips ¾" × WOF 4 strips ⅞" × WOF 12 strips 1" × WOF 7 strips 1⅛" × WOF 5 strips 1¼" × WOF 1 strip 1½" × WOF (Spiral 2 Center) 3 strips 2" × WOF (Outside edges of wedges) 1 strip 2¼" × WOF (Cut down to 8 Solid Cream template.) 4 Background Original (See cutting diagram on CD) 4 Background Reverse
Backing and Hanging Sleeve	Any	3¼ yds	(Note: If Borders are cut from the same fabric as Backing, 3¼ yds is enough for borders and backing.) Cut two 58" lengths, seam together for 58" × 58" Backing square. Cut 10" × 50" strip from leftover Backing for Hanging Sleeve.
Batting	52" × 52" square		
Translucent Foundation Sheets	32 sheets 8½" × 11"		
White Paper	19 sheets 8½" × 11"		

Templates and a fabric selection guide are on the CD accompanying this book. Read pages 96–97 before buying fabric. Follow the instructions found previously in this book to sew spirals and assemble the mandala. Instructions particular to this quilt are given on pages 136–137.

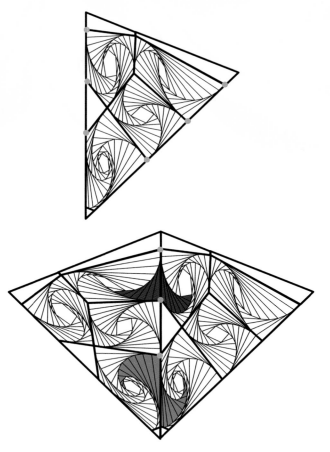

CUTTING FABRIC

Cut fabric according to the instructions outlined on pages 96–99 and 118, using the cutting templates on white paper. Cut the Solid Cream pieces to the shape of the template.

SEWING THE SPIRALS

All spirals are Nesting spirals. Follow instructions on pages 104–105 for sewing Nesting and Baravelle spirals. Instructions regarding centers of spirals combined with parts of Ring A are given on the templates. Read and follow these carefully.

ASSEMBLING THE WEDGES AND MANDALA

Even if you plan to leave in the foundation, remove the foundation at corners where seams intersect to reduce bulk after sewing one seam across the corner (see page 110).

1. Sew the spirals together into 8 wedges in the order shown below. Join Spirals 1, 2 and 4. Join Spiral 3 to Fill-In Triangle. Join the two groups with a "Y" seam (see page 109).

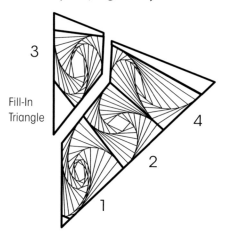

PREPARING FOUNDATIONS AND CUTTING TEMPLATES

There is only one wedge in this mandala—an asymmetrical wedge with matching side nodes used only in original orientation and set in rotational symmetry. Because the side nodes match, the flow forms connect smoothly from wedge to wedge.

Printing Templates

Print on white paper: 2 each of Spiral 1 through Spiral 4 foundations and Solid template. Keep one set of spirals as master templates and use the other set for cutting templates. Also print 1 set of Background templates and assemble Parts 1, 2 and 3.

Print on translucent foundation paper: 8 each of Spiral 1 through Spiral 4 foundations.

To Print Templates from EQ: In addition to the PDF version of this pattern, templates are also provided in EQ6. Before using the EQ file to make this quilt, read the file on this CD entitled "Using EQ Project Files." This contains important information that will impact the successful outcome of your project.

2. Sew background pieces to each wedge. (Notice that the background pieces are in mirror position but the wedges are not.)

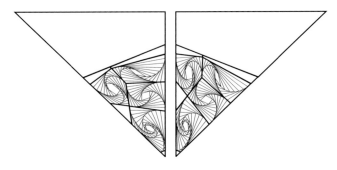

3. Join pairs of wedges into four large triangles. Sew a 50" border strip to the long side of each triangle. Center the border strips so that an equal amount of excess fabric extends out on from each end.

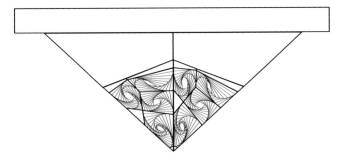

Alternately, if the border strips are 25¼" instead of 50" long, sew each border strip to a wedge before joining pairs of wedges. Then join the pairs of wedges aligning the Border seam.

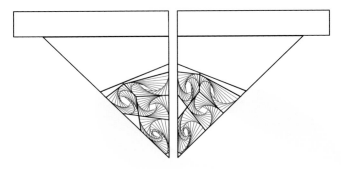

4. Sew the pairs of wedges into two halves of the quilt, then join the halves to complete the quilt. The borders will automatically miter when the quarters of the quilt are joined. Trim off excess border fabric from corner seams.

If you are removing the foundation, remove it all now. If you are leaving the foundation in, and you used tape to hold the fabric at the centers of the spirals, tear out the the foundation at the center of each spiral and remove the tape.

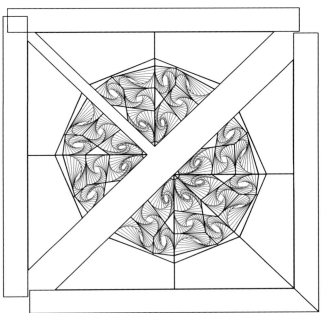

QUILT

Quilt as desired. If necessary, square up after quilting.

BINDING

This quilt uses a standard folded binding ½" wide. Join the binding strips with diagonal seams at the ends, then press in half lengthwise. Set the raw edges of the binding at the trimmed edge of the quilt and stitch a generous ¼" inside the raw edges of the binding. Turn the folded edge to the back and hand-stitch in place to finish. Complete illustrated instructions can be found on the CD that came with this book.

FINISH

Add a label and hanging sleeve, if desired.

CRIMES OF PASSION

Finished size: 54½" × 54½"; Mandala size: 20" radius (40" diameter)

The dark, masculine colors in this design remind me of Henry VIII, but the whole color scheme started with the pink and gold in the hearts, which put me in mind of Henry's passion for Anne Boleyn (at least until he had her beheaded).

I tried several colorings for this mandala. One morning after staying up too late watching the Showtime series *The Tudors*, this found its way onto my computer screen. This mandala uses the same wedge used in *That's The Way Love Is* on page 134. The difference? This design uses the wedge in both rotational symmetry and in mirror symmetry. In effect, the two wedges that make up each quarter are repeated in compound mirror symmetry.

What you'll learn in this mandala: Nesting spirals, rotational symmetry, mirror symmetry, compound mirror symmetry, solid flow forms, variegated flow forms, negative space, pieced background

COLOR (POSITION)	FABRIC TYPE	MIN. AMOUNT	CUTTING INSTRUCTIONS (READ PAGES 96-99 AND 118 BEFORE CUTTING)
Pink and Gold (Spirals)	Energy	½ yd	7 strips 1" × WOF 8 strips 1⅛" × WOF
Dark Red (Spirals)	Foundation	⅝ yd	16 strips 1" × WOF 2 strips 1¼" × WOF 1 strip 1¾" × WOF
Light Red (Spirals)	Foundation	⅜ yd	2 strips ¾" × WOF 2 strips 1" × WOF 4 strips 1¼" × WOF 2 strips 1½" × WOF
Red Swirl (Border) (Can be same Dark Red above)	Energy or Foundation	⅞ yd (Note: Borders are different in EQ and may require different yardage. Use fabric calculation in EQ to check.)	Cut from templates (Cut generously, then trim after sewing.) 4 Border 3 4 Border 3 reversed 4 Border 6 4 Border 6 reversed For EQ Borders: Cut 4 of each red Border strips and Corner block. Print templates from EQ.
Grey (Spirals)	Foundation	1 yd	2 strips ¾" × WOF 2 strips 1" × WOF 9 strips 1¼" × WOF 9 strips 1⅜" × WOF 2 strips 1½" × WOF 1 strip 2¼" × WOF
Black Speckles (Edge of Mandala)	Energy	¼ yd	1 strip 1¼" × WOF 2 strips 1¾" × WOF
Black (Spirals, Background, Border, Binding)	Foundation	3½ yds (Note: Borders are different in EQ and may require different yardage. Use fabric calculation in EQ to check.)	Cut in this order (see cutting diagram on page 140): 5 strips 2½" × WOF (binding) 4 Background 4 Background reversed 4 strips 1¼" × 60" (Border 7) 4 Border 2 4 Border 2 reversed 4 Border 4 4 Border 4 reversed 4 Border 5 4 Border 5 reversed For Spirals (total length strip in parentheses): 6 strips ¾" × WOF (220") 2 strips ⅞" × WOF (88") 11 strips 1" × WOF (440") 2 strips 1⅛" × WOF (88") 9 strips 1¼" × WOF (352") 5 strips 1⅜" × WOF (308")

COLOR (POSITION)	FABRIC TYPE	MIN. AMOUNT	CUTTING INSTRUCTIONS (READ PAGES 96-99 AND 118 BEFORE CUTTING)
Gold 1 (Spirals)	Energy	⅜ yd	2 strips 1⅛" × WOF 3 strips 1¼" × WOF 2 strips 1⅜" × WOF
Gold 2 (Spirals, Border)	Foundation	⅝ yd (Note: Borders are different in EQ and may require different yardage. Use fabric calcula-tion in EQ to check.)	14 strips 1¼" × WOF Cut 8 Border 1 from 8 of the strips. Use the remainder of these strips, plus the other 6 WOF strips for cutting triangles for spirals. See diagram below.
Backing and Hanging Sleeve	Any	3¼ yds	Cut two 58" lengths, seam together for 58" × 58" backing. Cut 10" × 50" strip from leftover backing. Hem each end, then sew into a tube for Hanging Sleeve. Attach to the back at the top edge of the quilt.
Batting	57" × 57" square		
Translucent Foundation Sheets	72 sheets 8½" × 11"		
White Paper	30 sheets 8½" × 11"		

Templates and a fabric selection guide are on the CD accompanying this book. Read pages 96–97 before buying fabric. Follow the instructions found previously in this book to sew spirals and assemble the mandala. Instructions particular to this quilt are given on pages 140–143.

Cutting diagram for Black

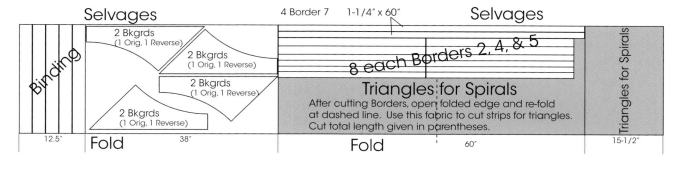

Cutting diagram for Gold 2

Borders in EQ: The borders in the PDF templates for this quilt are pieced, with a mitered corner. EQ does not allow a pieced, mitered border. So, the borders in the EQ version are "Corner Block" style and are slightly different from the PDF version. It is possible to use the PDF borders even if you make the rest of the quilt using EQ (provided it is the same size as the PDF templates). If you use the EQ borders, print EQ templates and cut from them.

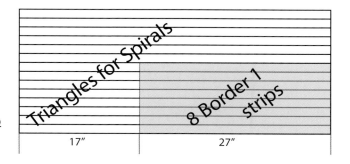

140

PREPARING FOUNDATIONS AND CUTTING TEMPLATES

This mandala uses a single AMSN wedge (the same one as *That's the Way Love Is*), but it is colored in two different variations; the wedges along the vertical axis (V and VR) and the wedges along the horizontal axis (H and HR) (see photo on page 138 and the diagram at right).

The same coloration of the wedge is placed in mirror symmetry along the vertical and horizontal axes.

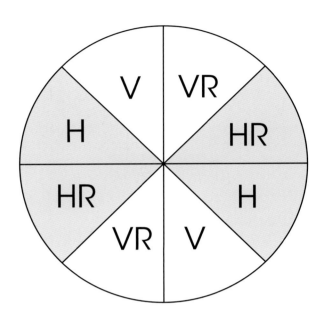

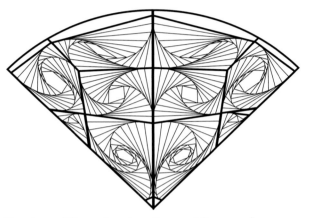

The two different colorations of the wedge are placed in rotational symmetry within the quarter of the design between the vertical and horizontal axes.

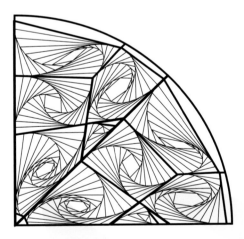

The templates provided are in original orientation. For reverse orientation, print the template on translucent foundation, turn it over and mark "R" on the back. This is now the front of the "Reverse" foundations. There is no need to make two sets of cutting templates because all fabric for spirals is cut as rectangular strips, not triangles; each strip will work in either original or reverse orientation.

Printing Templates

Print on white paper:
2 of each spiral foundation V1 through V5 and H1 through H5. Keep one set of spirals as master templates and use the other set for cutting templates. Assemble V1, H1, V4 and H4, Parts 1 and 2.
1 Background template. Assemble Background Parts 1, 2 and 3
1 Border template. Assemble Border Parts 1, 2 and 3.
Print on translucent foundation paper:
4 of each spiral foundation V1 through V5 and H1 through H5. Assemble V1, H1, V4 and H4, Parts 1 and 2. Turn over 2 of each spiral foundation and mark "R" or Reverse.
8 Border foundations. Assemble Parts 1, 2 and 3. Turn over 4 Border foundations and mark "R" for Reverse.
To Print Templates from EQ: In addition to the PDF version of this pattern, templates are also provided in EQ6. Before using the EQ file to make this quilt, read the file on this CD entitled "Using EQ Project Files." This contains important information that will impact the successful outcome of your project.

CUTTING FABRIC

Cut fabric according to the instructions outlined on pages 96–99 and 118, using the cutting templates on white paper.

SEWING THE SPIRALS

All spirals are Nesting spirals. Sew according to instructions on pages 104–105 for Nesting and Baravelle spirals. Additional instructions regarding sewing are given on the templates. Read and follow these carefully. Sew spirals in groups of 4, working with the same coloration of each spiral together.

SEWING THE BORDERS

Assemble the borders, sewing pieces in numerical order. Work in the same way as you would sew a spiral:

Place Border 1 in position with tape, then do a next step trim along both edges to set up seam allowances. Attach Border 2, aligning the edge of the cut strip with the edge of the next step trim on Border 1.

After sewing Border 2, do a next step trim on it to set up the seam allowance for Border 3. Repeat these steps for Border strips 3 through 6. Do not attach Border 7 at this time.

For EQ Borders, sew the Border strips as explained above. (There are only 5 sections, not 6.) After assembling the Border, attach half of the Corner block to the end of the Border strip. This creates the angle for a mitered corner when the wedges are joined. (Cut the corner triangle generously for "insurance" to miter the corner.)

EQ borders

ASSEMBLING THE MANDALA

Before sewing the spirals together, arrange the spirals and background pieces in their final positions. Look at the picture on page 138 for correct positioning. Even if you plan to leave in the foundation, remove the foundation at corners where seams intersect, to reduce bulk (see page 109).

1. Sew the spirals together into 8 wedges in the order shown below. Join Spirals 1, 2 and 4. Join Spirals 3 and 5. Join the two groups with a "Y" seam (see page 109). (Reverse wedges will be opposite of the position shown here.)

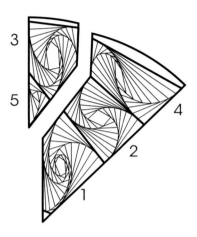

2. Arrange the wedges, background pieces and porders in their correct positions.

The wedges will pair up V+VR and HR+H (see the photo on page 138 and the diagam on page 141 for wedge placement).

Sew the background pieces to their corresponding wedges, using matching marks to align the curved edges.

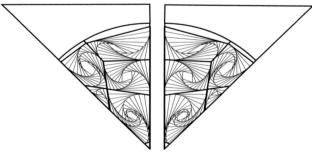

3. Sew each border strip to its corresponding wedge.

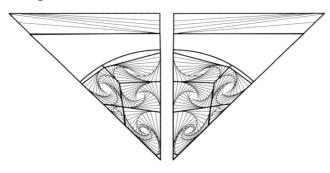

4. Join wedges into 4 pairs of triangles that make up the four sides of the quilt.

5. Attach Border 7 pieces (Border 3 for EQ) to the quarters.

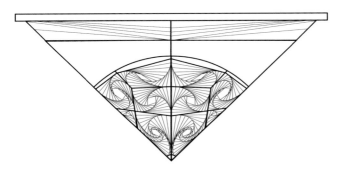

6. Join the quarters into halves, then the halves into a complete quilt, matching border seams. The borders will automatically miter when the quarters of the quilt are joined. Trim off any excess border fabric at the corners and press the seams open.

If you are removing the foundation, remove it all now. If you are leaving the foundation in, and you used tape to hold the fabric at the center of the spirals, tear out the foundation at the center of each spiral and remove the tape.

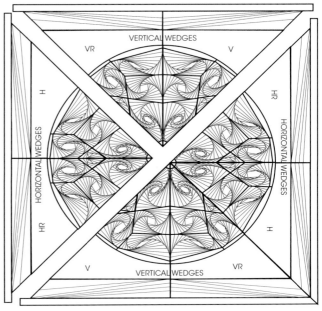

QUILTING

Quilt as desired. If necessary, square up after quilting.

BINDING

This quilt uses a standard folded binding ½" wide. Join the binding strips with diagonal seams at the ends, then press in half lengthwise. Set the raw edges of the binding at the trimmed edge of the quilt and stitch a generous ¼" inside the raw edges of the binding. Turn the folded edge to the back and hand-stitch it in place to finish. Complete illustrated instructions can be found on the CD that came with this book.

FINISH

Add a label and hanging sleeve, if desired.

143

SULTANA

Finished size: 54½" × 54½"; Mandala size: 22" radius (44" diameter)
Quilted by Diane Anderson

Sultana was the name on the selvage of the African fabric used as a jewelry fabric in this quilt . . . and the name seemed to fit.

This mandala uses a perfectly symmetrical wedge. Even the main spirals are symmetrical because they are Baravelle spirals that can spin in both directions. Careful color placement and gradations also give this design its three-dimensional feel. Throughout the design, colors are placed to look as though they pass under other layers of the design and reappear elsewhere. Gradations moving from light to dark away from the white centers of the spirals give the appearance that a strong light is shining through from behind the mandala. Tiny tone-on-tone prints give the entire mandala a shimmering, pointillistic effect. The fuchsia and coral stripes, as well as the red "tail" that swings off the Baravelle spirals toward the center, both result from subdividing corners of the large shape that contains the Baravelle spiral.

What you'll learn in this mandala: Nesting, Baravelle and hybrid spirals; steering a Pinwheel spiral; symmetrical wedge; T-joints; subdividing corners; solid, value gradation and variegated flow forms; flowunders; pieced background

144

COLOR (POSITION)	FABRIC TYPE	MIN. AMOUNT	CUTTING INSTRUCTIONS (READ PAGES 96-99 AND 118 BEFORE CUTTING)
Red (Spirals, Border 1, Binding)	Foundation	1½ yds	9 strips ¾" × WOF 8 strips ⅞" × WOF 12 strips 1" × WOF 3 strips 1⅛" × WOF 5 strips 1" × WOF (Border 1) 6 strips 2½" × WOF (Binding)
Coral 1 (Spirals)	Foundation	⅜ yd	3 strips ¾" × WOF 3 strips ⅞" × WOF 3 strips 1" × WOF 4 strips 1¼" × WOF
Coral 2 (Spirals)	Foundation	⅜ yd	6 strips ¾" × WOF 2 strips ⅞" × WOF 1 strip 1⅛" × WOF 2 strips 1⅜" × WOF
Coral 3 (Spirals)	Foundation	½ yd	3 strips ¾" × WOF 3 strips ⅞" × WOF 1 strip 1⅛" × WOF 2 strips 1¼" × WOF 5 strips 1⅜" × WOF
Seven shades of green in gradation from light to dark:			
Green 1 (Lightest) (Spirals)	Foundation	⅛ yd	12 squares 1" × 1"
Green 2 (Spirals)	Foundation	⅛ yd	3 strips ¾" × WOF 2 strips ⅞" × WOF 3 strips 1" × WOF 2 strips 1¼" × WOF (cut into 12 pieces 1½" × 1¼")
Green 3 (Spirals)	Foundation	⅛ yd	1 strip 1¼" × WOF 1 strip 1⅜" × WOF
Green 4 (Spirals)	Foundation	⅛ yd	2 strips 1½" × WOF
Green 5 (Spirals)	Energy or Foundation	¼ yd	1 strip 1⅛" × WOF 2 strips 1½" × WOF 2 strips 1⅝" × WOF
Green 6 (Spirals)	Energy	¼ yd	3 strips 1½" × WOF 3 strips 1⅜" × WOF
Green 7 (Darkest) (Spirals, Background)	Foundation	1¾ yds	2 strips 1¼" × WOF 3 strips 1⅜" × WOF 4 Background Corner 4 Background Side 4 Background Side reverse
Cream (Spirals)	Foundation	¼ yd	1 strip 1" × WOF 1 strip 1¼" × WOF 1 strip 1⅜" × WOF 1 strip 1¾" × WOF

COLOR (POSITION)	FABRIC TYPE	MIN. AMOUNT	CUTTING INSTRUCTIONS (READ PAGES 96–99 AND 118 BEFORE CUTTING)
Eight shades of gold in gradation from dark to light:			
Gold 1 (Darkest) (Spirals)	Foundation	¼ yd	1 strip 1¼" × WOF 1 strip 1" × WOF 2 strips 1¼" × WOF
Gold 2 (Spirals)	Foundation	⅛ yd	2 strips 1¼" × WOF
Gold 3 (Spirals)	Foundation	⅛ yd	2 strips 1¼" × WOF
Gold 4 (Spirals)	Foundation	⅛ yd	1 strip 1⅛" × WOF
Gold 5 (Spirals)	Foundation	¼ yd	1 strip ⅞" × WOF 2 strips 1" × WOF 1½ strips 1¼" × WOF
Gold 6 (Spirals)	Foundation	⅛ yd	1 strip ⅞" × WOF
Gold 7 (Spirals)	Foundation	⅛ yd	1 strip ⅞" × WOF
Gold 8 (Lightest) (Spirals)	Foundation	¼ yd	4 strips 1" × WOF 2 strips 1½" × WOF
Fuchsia	Foundation	¼ yd	2 strips 1" × WOF 3 strips 1¼" × WOF 2 strips 1⅝" × WOF
Fuchsia/Red Blend	Energy	¼ yd	4 strips 1¼" × WOF
Yellow	Foundation	⅜ yd	3 strips ¾" × WOF 1 strip ⅞" × WOF 1 strip 1⅛" × WOF 1 strip 1¼" × WOF 2 strips 1¾" × WOF
Gold Large-Scale Print (Border)	Jewelry	¼ yd (more if fussy cutting)	5 strips 1¾" × WOF
Focal Fabric	Jewelry	See note at right	Enough to cut 12 repetitions of motif for center star and 6 repetitions of motif for center of Middle spiral.
Backing & Hanging Sleeve	Any	3½ yds	63" square for backing. Cut 2 lengths 63" long. Sew together along selvages. Trim to 63" square. Cut a 9" × 55" strip for hanging sleeve from trimmed fabric.
Batting	56" × 56" square		
Translucent Foundation Sheets	54 sheets 8½" × 11"		
White Paper	20 sheets 8½" × 11"		

Templates and a fabric selection guide are on the CD accompanying this book. Read pages 96–97 before buying fabric. Follow the instructions found previously in this book to sew spirals and assemble the mandala. Instructions particular to this quilt are given on pages 147–149.

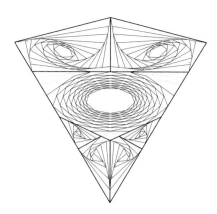

PREPARING FOUNDATIONS AND CUTTING TEMPLATES

This mandala is made up of 6 copies of the same wedge. Within the wedge there are four spirals: three spirals in mirrored pairs and one central spiral.

The three mirrored spirals are Side Spiral, Outer Spiral and Point Spiral. Side Spirals and Outer Spirals are colored the same in both Original and Reverse. In the Point Spiral, the coloring is different in Left and Right. The fourth spiral is the Middle spiral, the large Baravelle that bridges between both sides of the wedge.

Printing Templates

Print on white paper:
2 Outer and Side spirals. Assemble Parts 1 and 2 of Outer Spiral.
2 Middle Spiral. Assemble Parts 1, 2, 3 and 4
2 Point Left and Point Right spirals (they are on the same page)
1 Background Sides. Assemble Parts 1 and 2.
1 Background Corners. Assemble Parts 1, 2, 3 and 4
(Keep one set of spirals as master templates and use the other set for cutting templates.)
Print on translucent foundation paper:
12 Outer spirals and 12 Side spirals. Assemble Parts 1 and 2 of Outer Spiral. Turn over 6 Outer spirals and 6 Side spirals and mark them R or Reverse. This side is now the front.
6 Middle spirals. Assemble Parts 1, 2, 3 and 4;
6 Point Left spirals and 6 Point Right spirals.
To Print Templates from EQ: In addition to the PDF version of this pattern, templates are also provided in EQ6. Before using the EQ file to make this quilt, read the file on this CD entitled "Using EQ Project Files." This contains important information that will impact the successful outcome of your project.

CUTTING FABRIC

Cut fabric according to instructions on pages 96–99 and 118 using cutting templates on white paper.

SEWING THE SPIRALS

Before you start sewing, plan the position of all fussy-cut elements.

Sew 6 original orientation and 6 reverse of all spirals except Middle spiral. The Point spirals and Outer spirals are hybrid Nesting/Pinwheel spirals. Specific instructions for sewing them are printed on the template sheet. Read and follow these instructions carefully.

The Side spirals are Nesting spirals. The Middle spiral is a Baravelle spiral with subdivided corners. Follow the instructions for sewing Nesting and Baravelle spirals on pages 104–105.) Specific instructions for sewing the corners are printed on the template sheet. Read and follow these instructions carefully.

After sewing spirals, trim ¼" outside all edges of spirals for seam allowance.

ASSEMBLING THE WEDGES AND MANDALA

Even if you plan to leave in the foundation, remove the foundation at corners where seams intersect to reduce bulk after sewing one seam across the corner (see page 110).
1. Sew each Point Left spiral to a Side (Original) spiral. Sew each Point Right spiral to a Side (Reverse) spiral. Sew the center seam between the Point Left spiral and the Point Right spiral. If you want to eliminate the bottom of the center seam, use the Cut-off Point method (see page 83).

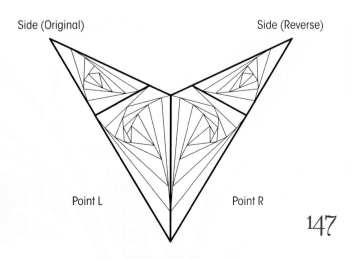

Side (Original)   Side (Reverse)

Point L   Point R

2. Sew the Point/Side assembly to the bottom of the Middle Spiral. There is a "Y" seam (a yellow dashed line in the illustration below).

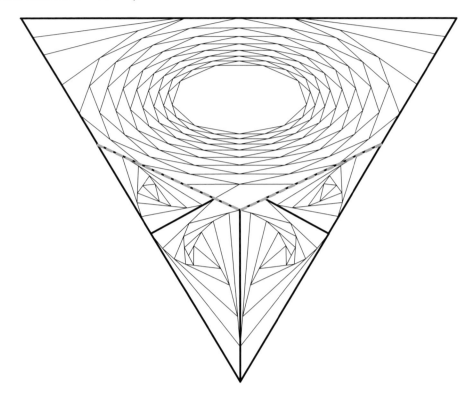

3. Arrange the assembled sections of the wedges, the Outer and Outer (Reverse) spirals, and the Background-Side and Background-Corner pieces in their final positions. (Refer to the diagram on the next page for position guidance.) Sew each Background piece to its corresponding Outer or Outer (Reverse) spiral.

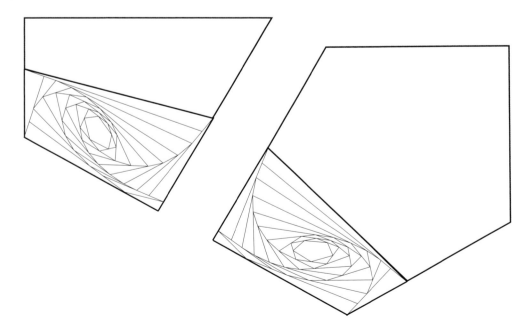

4. Join each pair of Outer spirals with their attached Background pieces, then join each Point/Side/Middle assembly to an Outer/Background assembly.

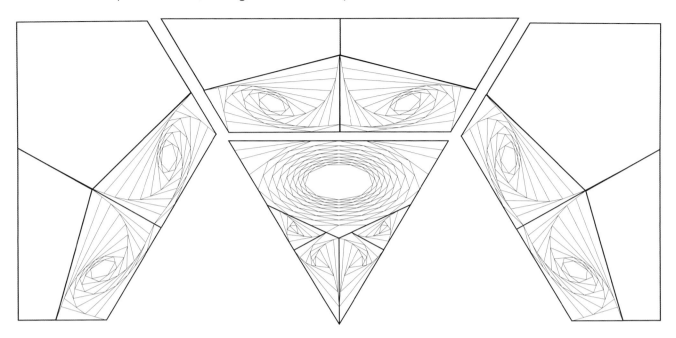

5. Join two groups of 3 wedges into two halves of the mandala, then join the halves to complete the mandala.

6. If necessary, square up the sides of the quilt top. Join Border 1 and Border 2 strips to make strips long enough for the borders.

Sew Border 1 strips (Red, 1" wide) to the sides of the quilt top. Trim the ends even with the edges of the quilt top. Sew Border 1 strips to the top and bottom of the quilt top. Trim the ends even with the edges of the previous border strips.

Sew Border 2 strips (Yellow, 1¾" wide) to the sides of the quilt top. Trim the ends even with the edges of the quilt top. Sew Border 2 strips to the top and bottom of the quilt top. Trim the ends even with the edges of the previous border strips.

If you are removing the foundation, remove it all now. If you are leaving the foundation in, and you used tape to hold the fabric in the centers of the spirals, tear out the foundation at the center of each spiral and remove the tape.

QUILTING

Quilt as desired. If necessary, square up after quilting.

BINDING

This quilt uses a standard folded binding ½" wide. Join the binding strips with diagonal seams at the ends, then press in half lengthwise. Set the raw edges of the binding at the trimmed edge of the quilt and stitch a generous ¼" inside the raw edges of the binding. Turn the folded edge to the back and hand-stitch it in place to finish. Complete illustrated instructions can be found on the CD that came with this book.

FINISH

Add a label and hanging sleeve, if desired.

GALLERY

Each of the quilts on these pages shows the creator applying mandala techniques in his or her own unique and creative way. Let their vision and sense of adventure inspire you!

The Zebras Went Crazy

Designed and pieced by Holly Watson, quilted by Gwen Baggett
8-wedge mandala, mirror symmetry
60" × 60"
Variegated flow forms in black and white contrast with gradation flow forms in warm jungle colors to create this whimsical African-themed quilt.

Harmony

Designed, pieced and quilted by
Betsy Vinegrad
10-wedge, rotational symmetry
23½" × 23½"
After completing *Cosmic Spin* (page 43), Betsy worked on this design for months. The entire area inside the yin and yang symbol is pieced as spirals; the most challenging part of the design was to get the motion of the flow forms in the outer areas to flow into the mandalas.

Rhythm of the Sun

Designed, pieced and quilted by Gill Drury
8-wedge, compound rotational symmetry
48" × 48"

Linked flow forms create the orange ribbons that swirl toward the center and back out again. The wedge skeleton is asymmetrical and set in mirror symmetry. In the wedge on the left, all three spirals spin clockwise. But, when the wedge is flipped, only one spiral flips into counterclockwise spin; the other two spirals still spin clockwise. This creates 2 different wedges set in compound symmetry.

Blue Birds of Paradise

Designed and pieced by Linda McGibbon, quilted by Carol Rose
10-wedge, mirror symmetry
59" × 59"

As Linda worked with this design, she saw birds flying toward its center. By coloring some of the wedges blue and some green, she separated the birds from what would otherwise be simply a pattern repeated around the mandala. Finding the blue bird fabric for the background was pure serendipity.

151

Renaissance Dreams

Designed, pieced and quilted by
Barbara Baker
8-wedge, compound mirror
symmetry
72" × 72"
This quilt uses the same wedge
as *Pepperoni, Mushrooms, Double
Cheese* on page 24, but what a
difference the fabric choices make!
Instead of filling the outer shapes
with spirals, Barbara fussy-cut the
border fabric to create an elegant
inner border around the mandala.

A Summer on Grant Island

Designed and pieced by Daniel Lundby,
quilted by Diane Anderson
8-wedge square, mirror symmetry
71½" × 71½"
Finding himself on a remote island without
a copier, Daniel hand-drew all of the
several dozen foundations for this quilt. As
he sewed, he accidentally reversed one
set of spirals and made them backward.
But, when he put the wedges together, he
discovered that the "mistake" made the
bows on each side, which he liked even
better than the original design.

There's a Rainbow in Here Somewhere...

Designed and pieced by Jamie McClenaghan,
quilted by Gwen Baggett
12-wedge, mirror symmetry
54" × 54"
One of the things I particularly love about this
mandala is the how the shimmery fabric floats
around the edge. Jamie created this effect
by "blacking out" sections of the spirals that
contain this fabric.

Acts 2:3

Designed, pieced, appliquéd and quilted
by Jill Kerekes
45" diameter
12-wedge
This unique mandala started with a
simple idea: place the center point
off-center. Because of this, each wedge
is different. All of the spirals spin in the
same direction, making all of the flow
forms trunks and giving the mandala the
feel of rotational symmetry. Jill colored
them yellow, orange and red to look like
flames.

Flow Blue

Designed, pieced and quilted by
Mary Cannizzaro
10-wedge, mirror symmetry
68" × 68"
Mary has a wonderful sense of
color, even when she is only using
one color. This very "cool" mandala
contains over 20 shades of blue
and several subtle shades of white
as well.

The Empowerment of Women

Designed, pieced, appliquéd and quilted by
Patty Martin
8-wedge, mirror symmetry
72" × 72"
Patty's color scheme was inspired by an
Asian floral fabric from which she also cut
the appliqués. The blue gradations in the
mandala and the background make the
entire design seem to glow from within. The
outermost triangle of each wedge is divided
into rays, rather than set with spirals, to
create the border.

154

I Think I'm Losing My Marbles

Designed, pieced and quilted by
Susan Ott
6-wedge, mirror and rotational symmetry
23" diameter
This quilt is a twin to *Blueberry Swirl Sundae* on page 71. Both quilts use the same wedge skeleton—the coloring and the directions of some of the spirals has changed.

Nova 1038

Designed, pieced and quilted by
Ruth Shadar
12-wedge, mirror symmetry
44" × 44"
Ruth included both spiral and non-spiral elements in this design to create a mandala that seems like a marriage between a spiral mandala and a Mariner's Compass. The title comes from the number of pieces.

Appendix

PHOTOCOPYING AND PHOTOGRAPHING YOUR MANDALA-IN-PROGRESS

As you design and make your spiral mandala quilt, you will frequently need to make copies of your sketches, templates and foundations. Although you can do this by hand, having access to a photocopier is essential as far as I'm concerned because it makes copying so much faster and easier. You will also want to take photographs of mandala designs as you work with the hinged mirrors. Here are some pointers:

PHOTOCOPIERS AND PRINTERS

If you have a home computer, I strongly recommend that you get an all-in-one printer/scanner/photocopier. Look for one that will make mirror-image copies (often it's a feature called "Photo Transfer"). Printers like this can cost less than $100, and if you can't find one at an office supply store near you, they can be ordered at reputable online sites. This will save you many trips to a copy shop! Even if you have a copier at your office, it's good to have one at home, so you don't have to stop in the middle of a burst of inspiration on Saturday to wait to use the photocopier at the office on Monday.

If you work in a graphic design program such as Photoshop, CorelDRAW or Illustrator, another advantage of this type of printer is that it enables you to scan your sketches and fabric swatches. The scanned images can then be imported into your graphic design program, where you can copy, rotate, flip, color and print your designs.

Mirror-Image Copies

If you already have a photocopier, but it does not have a mirror-image copy function, use one of these methods to make reverse copies:

- Print or photocopy your drawing onto translucent foundation paper. Turn the copy over and mark the back "Reverse." This is your reverse master. Make all your reverse copies from this master. (Since copies made from this master are actually second-generation copies, you may run into distortion problems. If so, use the next method, which eliminates one generation of copying.)

- Begin with your drawing or sketch on plain white paper (don't reuse paper that has been printed on one side). Tape it to a window or light box with the drawing side away from you. Carefully trace the drawing onto the back of the paper and mark this side "Reverse." Photocopy this side when you need a reverse image of your original drawing.

Compounding Copies

When making copies of a wedge to design a mandala, you don't need to make a copy for each wedge. Save time, money, paper and the environment by compounding copies. To do this, make the first 2 copies of your wedge and join them together. Then, make a copy of the combined wedges. Add that to the one you copied from—now you have 4 wedges. Make a copy of these 4 combined wedges—now you have 8 wedges. Continue combining copies until you have the number of wedges you need.

PRINTER & PHOTOCOPIER ERROR

It is not unusual for photocopiers and printers—particularly inkjet printers—to print with inaccurate dimensions in at least one direction. This happens because the paper has to travel through a series of rollers, and as it does, it can shift back and forth or drag due to friction.

It's a good idea to copy or print a test template and measure it to see if it's the correct size. However, with irregularly shaped templates this is not always possible. A more accurate test is to print the templates and fit them together as explained on page 87.

One way to minimize the possibility of distortion is to make all the copies for your foundations on the same printer or photocopier (at the same time) so any distortion will at least be consistent across all copies.

Also, avoid making copies from copies, as distortion will compound from generation to generation.

If there is distortion, you can ignore it if it's consistent in all the templates and they still fit, or if the difference is small enough (less than ⅛") that it can be compensated for by the flexibility of fabric.

If the difference in dimension is too large, first try printing on another printer, or even from another computer. If the templates still need adjustment, follow the instructions on page 87 to adjust them manually. Or, if you are working from a graphics program on the computer, you may be able to adjust the size of the template slightly to compensate for distortion.

The document on the CD entitled "Printing Instructions—Read before printing templates" gives more detail on distortion and what to do about it.

PHOTOGRAPHING MANDALAS IN THE MIRRORS

Work in a well-lit area, with the light source placed above the mirrors to avoid shadows on your drawing. Stand the mirrors on the sketch so that you can see the complete mandala in the mirrors.

To take a photo, position the camera at about a 45 degree angle to the mirrors and the tabletop. Adjust the camera angle as necessary so you can see the complete mandala in the viewfinder; the camera should not be aimed straight at the mirrors.

Once you are in position, take the picture. Try it both with a flash and without a flash. If you use a flash, and get a flare in the mirror, it is because the flash was aimed straight at the mirror, and the light bounced straight back into the camera. To avoid this, make sure the camera is at an angle to the mirrors.

If you are working indoors with the lights on and you don't use flash, you may get a yellowish or greenish cast to your photographs. The yellowish cast is caused by tungsten light bulbs; the greenish cast is caused by florescent light bulbs. Most digital cameras are pre-set to adjust for this automatically, but if yours isn't, check the owner's manual for instructions to put your camera on "tungsten" or "florescent" setting. And don't forget to change it back to normal when you're done!

Resources

TOOLS AND MATERIALS

Many of the tools and materials that I use in this book can be purchased at your local fabric store, your favorite online retailer, or in my online store, www.ranaemerrillquilts.com.

WORKSHOPS

Visit www.ranaemerrillquilts.com for more information about in-person and online workshops.

Index

Take your quilting to the next level. . .

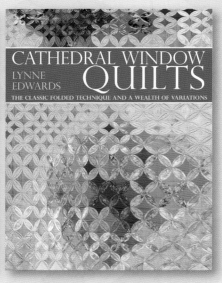

SIMPLY AMAZING SPIRAL QUILTS
RaNae Merrill

Enrich and expand the techniques found in *Magnificent Spiral Mandala Quilts* with RaNae's first book on spiral quilt design. Create fascinating and beautiful art quilts, learn to create five spiral-based quilts and master surprisingly easy techniques to create your own spiral designs—all with no math! The accompanying CD includes over 100 spiral templates in a variety of shapes and sizes.

paperback; 8¼" × 10⅞"; 160 pages
ISBN-10: 0-89689-653-6
ISBN-13: 978-0-89689-653-6
SRN: Z2049

BARGELLO QUILTS WITH A TWIST
Maggie Ball

This block-based technique for creating geometric bargello quilts eliminates the frustration of dealing with complex freeform patterns and large fabric strips in traditional bargello piecing. Fifteen projects in a variety of sizes and styles will show you how fun it can be to create bargello quilts by arranging blocks instead of fabric strips.

paperback; 8¼" × 10⅞"; 160 pages
ISBN-10: 0-89689-597-1
ISBN-13: 978-0-89689-597-3
SRN: Z1629

CATHEDRAL WINDOW QUILTS
Lynne Edwards

Internationally renowned quilt designer Lynne Edwards returns to this beautiful patchwork technique in *Cathedral Window Quilts*. Lynne's uniquely creative and accessible approach brings Cathedral Window quilting up to date and will capture your imagination and inspire you to learn and enjoy this technique and its variations.

paperback; 8¼" × 11"; 144 pages
ISBN-10: 0-7153-2713-5
ISBN-13: 978-0-7153-2713-5
SRN: Z2423

These and other fine Krause Publications titles are available at your local craft retailer, bookstore or online supplier, or visit our Web site at www.mycraftivitystore.com.